ADDITIONAL PRAISE FOR
STILL STANDING

The performance of every business leader hinges on their ability to respond quickly and clearly. *Still Standing* gives leaders the ability to adapt by using their most underutilized asset: tough conversations.

—**Dan Martell,** *Wall Street Journal*
best-selling author of *Buy Back Your Time*

A clear, clarion call for high performers to focus on the resilient, powerful skills that matter. It's time to open the door to connection, care, and humanity.

—**Seth Godin,** *New York Times*
best-selling author of *Linchpin* and *The Dip*

Still Standing was written with entrepreneurs and leaders in mind. A practical resource, this book gives leaders the tools to thrive and to lean into the tough conversations that unlock our greatness.

—**Giovanni Marsico,** three-time Emmy-winning
producer and Founder and CEO at Archangel

Still Standing is needed at a time when business leaders, especially founders, are navigating tough times. Being a founder is a rollercoaster ride, and in the most difficult times, there are few resources available. This book is genuine, uplifting, but most of all, empowering to those who need more real talk in their lives.

—**Bedy Yang,** Managing Partner at 500 Global

This book is an important contribution to our innovation ecosystem. Cherry Rose gives business leaders the actionable frameworks to build their resilience, so they can thrive in the workplace for years to come.

—**Brice Scheschuk,** Managing Partner at Globalive Capital and
Co-Founder and CFO at WIND Mobile

Having spent over 20 years as an entrepreneur, operator, and now VC, I can attest to the critical importance of workplace mental health, and yet how often this is overlooked or brushed aside. *Still Standing* is an honest and compassionate look at the conversations founders and leaders need to have today to ensure long-term health and vitality.

—**Janet Bannister,** Founder and Managing Partner at Staircase Ventures

Managing trauma and its impact on decision-making is increasingly the issue of our time. We have more tools available than ever before, yet the need has never been greater. Still Standing is a thoughtful dive into leadership mental health… a must read for all aspiring entrepreneurs.

—**Bruce Croxon,** Managing Partner at Round13 Capital and Co-Founder and CEO at Lavalife

STILL STANDING

STILL STANDING

WHAT IT TAKES TO THRIVE AND INNOVATE IN A MESSY WORLD

CHERRY ROSE TAN

WILEY

Published by John Wiley & Sons, Inc., Hoboken, New Jersey.
Published simultaneously in Canada.

For general information on our other products and services or for technical support, please contact
our Customer Care Department within the United States at (800) 762-2974, outside the United States
at (317) 572-3993 or fax (317) 572-4002.

Wiley also publishes its books in a variety of electronic formats. Some content that appears in print
may not be available in electronic formats. For more information about Wiley products, visit our web
site at www.wiley.com.

Library of Congress Cataloging-in-Publication Data is Available:

ISBN 9781394279029 (Cloth)
ISBN 9781394279043 (ePDF)
ISBN 9781394279036 (ePUB)

Cover Design: Wiley|Concept: Bill Falloon

SKY10085604_092324

To my dearest Keane,
the greatest entrepreneur
of all time

CONTENTS

CONTENTS

FOREWORD

As a venture capitalist, co-founder of multiple companies, and a startup community builder, I have experienced the unique challenges a founder faces on their journey. Tech founders have a unique job: to be the leaders creating and building the companies of the future. Over the past three decades, I have worked with and invested in numerous early-stage companies, and I believe deeply that founders need a startup community that supports them.

In early 2023, Cherry Rose reached out to me and asked if I would walk alongside her and contribute a foreword to her book, which is resolute and earnest in its stand on workplace mental health. More importantly, it is her deep belief that the lessons of this book will not only support and lift founders, but leaders of all organizations who are now faced with navigating the treacherous waters of innovation.

I currently host a podcast called *Give First* with my close friend and Techstars co-founder David Cohen, where, among other things, we discuss the importance of being positive and influential members of the innovation ecosystem. During the pandemic, I worked with the team at Techstars to produce the short documentary *Entrepreneurship & Mental Health*, which included a segment on my struggles with anxiety and depression. We do this because we know that founders and leaders struggle with mental health, often in silence, due to the stigma associated with mental health in the workplace.

Cherry Rose's book matters. Our industry is one of trailblazers: making bold moves and trying to change the status quo. During this journey, many founders face the most difficult challenges in their lives.

Working with tens of thousands of founders, Cherry Rose found that the answer reveals itself. We can become better, even thriving leaders, by mastering the art and science of tough conversations. Real talk is the key to creating an innovation economy where founders and leaders ask for help when needed. Real talk is the key to destigmatizing mental health and recognizing that most leaders will go through at least one adverse mental health experience during their careers. Real talk is the key to building adaptive and resilient leaders who set the example and strengthen our innovation economy.

In this book, you will find that you are not alone and will discover a way forward. This conversation on real talk and tough conversations may make the difference between a founder or leader who rises to the occasion and one who crashes and burns. Cherry Rose provides a step-by-step system that business leaders can apply and scale so that they and their organizations can thrive and succeed.

I hope the words and stories on these pages move and inspire you. Cherry Rose's book cuts through the noise because of her authenticity and bravery. She's had her own lived experience but has also been in the trenches with the thousands of tech leaders who have struggled with mental health, enabling her to convey the tools and the lessons that empower every leader to thrive and innovate in a messy world.

Whether you are a first-time founder or a veteran leader, *Still Standing* is a must-read. This book will challenge you to be honest with yourself, embrace your humanity, and lead with empathy and strength.

—Brad Feld, Partner at Foundry and Co-Founder at Techstars

INTRODUCTION

A few years ago, I sat with the CEO of a very successful, publicly listed company. This individual was wise beyond their years, weathered over the decades spent as a CEO. I will never forget the words they said, "If there is anything you need to do, anything you need to say, Cherry Rose, it is to tell entrepreneurs that trauma is inevitable. Loss is inevitable. Pain is inevitable. I wish I knew that going in so that I could have been kinder to myself."

After experiencing my own trauma, loss, and pain, I was inspired to create #REALTALK, the mental health movement for the tech industry. I have dedicated the last five years of my life to this work. I traveled around the world, holding space for over 40 000 leaders as we cried, laughed, and connected over our victories and our demons. Then I met some incredible founders, who are now dear friends and who encouraged me to tell my story and share my message with all of you.

Writing this book has been the most difficult, yet most rewarding experience of my life. It has been triggering and confronting, as I process my trauma and live by example. I have spent the last several years cleaning up my life to bring you the book that lies in your hands.

This book is not therapy. This book is not treatment.

But what this book can be is the *first step* – a shared space and under-standing of the ups and downs of entrepreneurship and innovation. It can be an admission, an acceptance that it is okay to struggle and that you aren't alone. You are not any less of a human, of a business leader, just because you struggle.

In this book, I invite you to keep an open mind. Allow your walls to come down and know that you are in a safe space. At #REALTALK, we are experts at what we do. We are founders first, with a deep desire to help our own. We know you because we have raised money, scaled companies, and dealt with the chaos of bankruptcies, lawsuits, defamations, and the good old drama of personal and professional stress.

As leaders of the future, our ability to create and transform industries is dependent on our stand – on our ability to say yes, to go all in, and to declare a possibility that others deem crazy. It is my stand that this book ends up in the hands of every business leader who is determined to survive and even thrive in these challenging times. I wish for real talk, the decency to be honest and there for one another, to live in the hearts and minds of every business leader who is committed to this path. To know that when you are struggling, when you find yourself at rock bottom, I, our champions, and our community will be there.

We have been where you are and we can help.

We will take a journey curated for you, inspiring you to build and lead in these changing times. This book is your safe haven, your eye in the storm.

Let's begin.

CHAPTER ONE

WHY #REALTALK?

I t was 26 December 2017, and it was the worst day of my life. Something was wrong. I could feel it in my bones. I woke up that day with a sense of dread. Inexplicable, stomach-turning dread.

For the last 48 hours, I had been trying to reach my little brother, Keane. Keane was my only sibling, and I missed him. We owned a Canadian blockchain company, a first mover in the space, that provided infrastructure and liquidity to global financial markets. I was involved as an early investor and Keane was its co-founder and chief operating officer.

Even though there was a fierce determination to make this company work, entrepreneurship was hard. Really hard. Keane was working long hours, the 100-hour weeks familiar to tech founders. It was workaholism – a common and even expected condition in the tech industry. A few weeks prior, Keane said he would be harder to reach. The year was ending and there was a frenzy to complete as much as possible before we saw each other for the holidays.

Despite our busy lives as sibling entrepreneurs, Keane and I had an unsaid agreement. Even though we were constantly busy and stressed, we always made time for each other when the other asked. *Always.* It was nonnegotiable. We made time for the things that mattered, like birthdays and tough times.

That day felt bizarre. Multiple people, from our mum to his best friend, were sending texts and calls to Keane. I left so many messages that day: texts, Facebook messages, WhatsApp messages, and phone calls. No one heard back and everyone was worried.

Keane was nowhere to be found. Everyone was wondering, *Was Keane okay? Where was he? Had something happened to him?* I had this weird, unsettling feeling that was building in my stomach.

Something was wrong. We needed to do something *now.*

I ended up calling his building and talking to a security guard. They knocked on his door to see if he was home. No answer. They guessed that Keane was outside, shopping on Boxing Day like many others in the city.

At that moment, I had a visceral reaction in my body, a whisper that said, "No, he's in there. I don't know how or why I know this, but he's in there." I asked them to open his door and they refused. I wasn't listed as his emergency contact. What was I going to do?

With one choice left, I called the police.

No one could have prepared me for what I saw. I remember rushing my way downtown with my parents and seeing paramedics and police surround his building. Watching the red and blue lights, the night felt so loud yet so silent at the same time. I ran to the elevators ahead of my parents, who were parking the car. I was trying to see what was happening.

As the elevator doors opened, I ended up on Keane's floor. Running toward his condo, I was stopped immediately. In the hallway stood a police officer with a solemn look on his face. The officer told me he was so sorry.

"Your brother is gone," he said.

Keane was gone. He had passed away in his sleep on Christmas.

THE DARK NIGHT OF THE SOUL

I share this experience of loss with you because, for many years, I grappled with my dark night of the soul and the aftermath that ensued across my family, our friends, and the tech industry.

Keane passed away from massive and sudden organ failure, a combination of prolonged overwork (120 hours a week, in fact) and a misdiagnosed condition. What do you do with that?

At the time of writing this book, the planet has been ravaged by the COVID-19 pandemic, followed by the economic recession. For the first time in decades, our planet is collectively grieving as millions of loved ones have passed away: sons and daughters, fathers and mothers, and even friends. So rarely, when we need the support the most, do we allow ourselves to be seen. So rarely, when we are struggling in the darkness, do we allow ourselves to be heard.

When was the last time you were able to be real with someone?

In this book, in this journey we share together, you are safe. You are seen. I wrote this book for people like you and people like me, who are navigating this messy world. I wrote this book for the business leaders of the future, the bold and the ambitious, who are innovating and building the new world we live in. Leaders, founders, and entrepreneurs who seem indestructible on the outside, but are just as human as everyone else.

This book is your eye in the storm, a space to return and rest when you need it.

In the media today, the game of innovation is glamorized. We celebrate the founders, the money they have raised, and the companies they have sold, but rarely do we see the journey it took to get them there. The sweat, the tears, the times when we doubted ourselves. The things we lost as we chose work and the pursuit of success over relationships, safety, and even our own health.

Innovation is an all-in sport. It is intense, emotional, and confronting for even the strongest of leaders.

As a serial entrepreneur, I am often hired by clients around the world as an innovation and mental health speaker: to share my real and hard-won experiences in navigating the game of innovation. This game includes exponential technologies like artificial intelligence (AI), blockchain, and metaverse, where all corporations, associations, and even universities are feeling the pressure to catch up. It is in these high-pressure, high-stakes environments that our workplaces are suffering.

Regular folks are struggling to make ends meet, and there is a general level of discontent (or as my clients like to call it, "rage") that has resulted from years of prolonged suffering on multiple levels: physical, mental, emotional, financial, and political. Regular folks are trying to find their way in this weird and wacky world, while being faced with the real and looming threat that their jobs and their livelihood can disappear at any second due to layoffs, offshoring, or even AI. In such a pressure cooker where so many of us feel the need to be excellent and to stand out to survive, the ability to share our true selves with others has lessened over time.

In working with many of my students as a university professor, I see them struggle to pause or even admit to needing help for fear of losing out on an opportunity or showing weakness. These pressures are at the individual level and also occur in teams and finally organizations, who are facing the largest wave of uncertainty they have seen yet: the extinction of 300 million jobs this decade due to AI.

How do you operate in a world of never-ending stress and change? How can we still stand as leaders, despite struggle after struggle?

MY WHY

Back in 2019, I ended up at a private event hosted by Jayson Gaignard, who founded the company MastermindTalks. His community of entrepreneurs is one of the most exclusive masterminds in the world, attracting 8- to 10-figure entrepreneurs and thought leaders from various industries.

At a restaurant in downtown Toronto, I met Tucker Max, a four-time *New York Times* best-selling author. As we chatted privately, our conversation became emotional. I had been following Tucker's work because he was public about his own struggles as an entrepreneur and how deep-seated trauma (and his subsequent healing journey) had affected his life. Being with Tucker, I remember leaning in and sharing my story. My story of what I had lived through and lost.

It took the 20 years of trauma that I had experienced and the 15 years of healing I had done prior, in order to have that conversation with him.

I told him that I was running #REALTALK, the mental health movement for the tech industry – my most important work yet – a platform for entrepreneurial stories, resources, and support through executive training, peer circles, and podcast interviews. Like the name of this movement, our superpower was talking: I was spending my days, fresh from my brother's death, sitting with tech CEOs and realizing that I wasn't alone in my lived experience. I was having mental health conversations with friends and colleagues in tech and it surprised me. There were so many of us who had struggled with mental health.

In those rooms, behind closed doors, these conversations opened a floodgate in my heart. These conversations felt tender and precious; despite the successes of these business leaders, they had struggled with depression, grief, addiction, and more.

In being with Tucker that night, he told me in no uncertain terms that I needed to write this story. That there are leaders we have lost in our families or in our circles due to mental illness and suicide. That this book could be the difference to the business leaders standing on the edge.

I know you, fellow leader, because I was one of those people.

When I lost my brother, my only sibling, I was confronted by my existence and the experiences I had lived. Before #REALTALK, I would walk into every room, thinking that I was alone. Despite being respected in my personal and professional circles, I felt like no one understood me. I had the accolades and the degrees, but no one knew the intensity of my despair.

I was a Filipino-Chinese Canadian and a first-generation immigrant. I was a Woman of Color (often the only one in the room), surrounded by other C-Suite leaders. As much as our industry pushes to be progressive, we have a long way to go. For instance, 7 to 10% of all venture capitalists are women, yet 52% of them are White men. This stat matters because career opportunities and upward mobility are dependent on who makes the decisions and who holds financial power. When we look at tech founders who are venture-backed, less than 1% are Women of Color, with 0.32% being Latinx founders and 0.0006% being Black founders.[1]

I share this context because the impact of mental health and trauma can feel absolute. Mental health impacts every part of our personal and professional lives, and it has a disproportionate impact on those who are already underrepresented.

When I began in the tech industry, in the game of innovation, I came as a trauma survivor. I was young, but I had already lived through so much, being surrounded by years of abuse, trauma, and mental illness. I had a family history that was rich with entrepreneurship yet steeped in painful experiences around colonization, war, and poverty from the Philippines.

By the time I came into this world, the odds were already stacked against me.

Even though I have suffered great losses, I understand that I am lucky. I could have ended up a statistic like my late brother, but I survived. Thrived even. In my grief, I was able to create a platform like #REALTALK and turn something horrific into something beautiful in this world.

I know Keane would be proud.

Through the unexpected ups and downs of life, we can choose to do better. We can say: It is time to support our own. It is time to see this book in the hands of every business leader and for them to know they are not alone.

FOR FOUNDERS, BY FOUNDERS

In the early days of our movement, there was pushback. Lots of pushback.

Our branding was particular, aimed at tech founders and only tech founders. People would approach me at events and say, "Why is #REALTALK for the tech industry? Why isn't #REALTALK for everyone?" As a trauma survivor myself, I know many industries and many communities struggle with mental health.

People found our obsession with tech founders *very* peculiar.

Many people assumed that #REALTALK was influenced by Keane's death, but the stakes are much more than that.

It is my deepest belief, being one of you and building the companies of the future, that business leaders of all walks of life can change the world. It sounds cheesy, but it's true. Despite what I have lived, I am lucky that I discovered entrepreneurship and innovation at such a young age.

When I was a little girl, I didn't know better. I didn't know that I was an anomaly or that my upbringing was unique, sitting at the dining table with Keane and our parents as they asked us what business idea we wanted to build next.

In every great loss I have ever experienced, I have created a company or a community to solve that problem.

In seeing how the tech industry has evolved in just a decade, we are the future. Technology is the future, not just for the founders, but for every industry on the planet. The business leaders of the future, individuals like yourself, are some of the biggest dreamers I know, declaring their moonshots and building their literal or figurative rockets to the moon. Each of us has so much potential, so much to give to the world, but we forget that.

We forget our roots and our why. Most importantly, we forget our hearts.

Our decisions and the way we lead can harm or inspire the people around us. In climbing the very steep hill that is building #REALTALK, I am certain that we can do better. That we must and can support our own, especially when leaders are stumbling in the darkness that is mental health. I know that being a leader in these times is tough, but we don't have to do it alone.

We can be friends. We can be allies. We can speak out and reconnect leader to leader. That was the vision of my late brother, who built and left his legacy in his own way.

Back in 2014, Keane was fresh out of university and working at one of the best mobile development firms in North America. When summer came, he flew with his close friend to Cape Town.

That trip was a big deal for him. Growing up as first-generation immigrants, we were poor. It was only when we were adults, making money from our jobs and our businesses, that we could afford to travel outside of North America.

He desired to see the world.

When he arrived in Cape Town, he noticed something: his entire itinerary was full of tourist traps, rather than authentic experiences to meet and understand the people who lived there. At the last minute, he changed his itinerary and booked a local guide, who arranged for him to stay in the villages. These villages were far away from the glamorous hotels. These were the villages where many of the locals stayed.

In the village that hosted him, Keane's life would be forever changed. In the weeks he stayed there, what moved Keane were the South African people who were entrepreneurs. Business leaders just like you and me, who have a dream. Who utilize their gifts to create something from nothing.

As Keane often reminded me for years to come, they were the *original entrepreneurs. The original founders.*

He admired them for their tenacity and resourcefulness, the way they used their hands and their lands to build goods. As he got to know them,

This is my brother Keane from this trip. He reminds me why #REALTALK stands *for founders, by founders.*

there was one person who stood out: a grandmother. She had lived in this village her whole life and her presence was formidable. For decades, she would weave baskets by hand and then travel many miles by foot, selling these baskets to neighboring villages. Afterward, she would save every piece of money from those sales, allowing her to purchase her first house years later.

In her example, she embodied a *glimpse:* an opening, an image showing what was possible for every other person in her village. It was her heart and her devotion to a better life that inspired Keane to become a founder.

In the same way that she was a glimpse for her village, Keane wanted to be a glimpse for her and all of the other entrepreneurs who dreamt of a better life. She reminded him so much of our ancestors, who experienced colonization, war, and poverty. Humble roots across generations, my ancestors planted the entrepreneurial seeds for our lineage and cultivated these seeds into successful businesses.

Keane saw this woman's potential.

It was his belief, our belief, that entrepreneurs like her deserved equal access to opportunities – that it didn't have to be so hard. In Canada, we are fortunate that services like banks are just a walk away. In that village and many regions like it, there are no physical banks for miles around. Banks didn't build in those places because they didn't see those individuals as "profitable" customers.

Was there a way to empower her, leader to leader?

It is this glimpse, a world *for founders, by founders*, that birthed our journey into blockchain.

THE LONE WOLF

We are more connected and disconnected than ever. I know this sentence to be true because of the 40 000 leaders we have worked with at #REALTALK.

In many ways, my experiences have led me here. A potent combination of a trauma survivor, psychology expert, and tech founder has led me to you. #REALTALK started organically from the need to be connected, knowing that as business leaders we could *and* will support our own.

In technology, we are heading there. Coming from the world of blockchain, Trust (with a capital T) is significant. Blockchain is a record-keeping technology that was built to restore and secure Trust, restoring functionality and progress in people and institutions where power and money reside. Blockchain and crypto have made their mark on the world because inherent in their nature is the ability for stakeholders to engage with each other, even in initial conditions where there is low or no trust amongst individuals. When you make a transaction, blockchain is what serves as the discerning and vetting intermediary, protecting both sides from harm. It is this trust that allows people to transfer and invest their money at whatever level they wish to participate. It is this trust that is the bedrock of our financial systems for the twenty-first century.

I share this observation because, unlike blockchain, our interactions with humans lack this foundation. We lack trust in one another, and thus, we are lonely.

We operate like lone wolves.

We live in a world where instead of connecting with others, we pretend. Our social media feeds are examples of how hard we try to hide and show people that our world is perfect. It is this foundation that has led to other trends like cancel culture and fake news.

Despite our technological advances, we are the *loneliest* we have ever been.

In a 2020 study, health insurer Cigna found a 13% rise in loneliness since 2018. Surveying 10 000 adult workers, they found that 63% of men are lonely and 58% of women are lonely.[2] This trend is increasing with every generation too: Gen Z (18–22 years old) reporting the highest loneliness average, with Boomers having the lowest.

Not only are we facing a dramatic increase in loneliness from a generational perspective, but it is occurring in our entrepreneurs as well. For instance, Startup Snapshot conducted a 2023 study focused on North American tech founders and found that founders spend 60% less time with spouses, 58% less time with kids, and 73% less time with friends and family.[3] Despite the hype around startups and the latest technologies like metaverse and AI, entrepreneurs are facing an average level of loneliness at 7.6/10.

The path to success can and has been incredibly painful for many. In a world of pretend, we have eroded trust completely. With the erosion of trust is the erosion of our dignity, connection, and support of other human beings, and a standard in the workplace where every person is left to fend for themselves, lucky if they survive. What is even more troubling about this growing pattern is that when I speak to audiences around the world, all companies from now until the foreseeable future are *tech* companies.

No company will be able to survive in the long run without being able to innovate. No company will be able to ignore the effects of technologies like blockchain, artificial intelligence, augmented reality (AR), and more.

Instead of allowing our people to drown in the workplace, unable to keep up with modern-day pressures and technologies, we need to come together. We need to create a shared language to acknowledge the difficult realities of the workplace, so that ourselves and others can feel safe to drop the mask. To stop pretending and operating as lone wolves.

What is a world without trust? What is a world without real talk?

THE GLIMPSE OF #REALTALK

When I talk to strangers, the most common question I get asked is, "How did #REALTALK start?"

In my world of startups and venture capital, we are inundated with the mythical figure of the founder, akin to an entrepreneurial superhero. Instead, my dive into #REALTALK was humbling, messy, and profoundly human.

Right after Keane's death, I was in huge amounts of pain. Not just physical pain or emotional pain, but *spiritual* pain. I was questioning everything about the fundamentals of life, principles that I once saw as resolute. I was questioning my purpose, my family, and my career. I had stayed awake for three *entire* days, my body in shock and heartbreak.

I couldn't sleep. I went from being an older sister, building companies with Keane for 10 years, to being an only child.

It destroyed me.

What was worse was the onslaught of struggles, of uphill battles, that came.

I was organizing my brother's funeral of 400 people and writing the eulogy. I was creating his Celebration of Life video and pouring through thousands of his pictures and videos; it was heartbreaking. My mother, who was grieving, was diagnosed with Stage 3C cancer less than two weeks after Keane's death.

She got the news four days before the funeral.

The company that Keane and I shared felt the loss too. His best friend was its co-founder and CEO, and the leadership team was like family to Keane. In the aftermath of losing their co-founder and COO, there was so much personal and professional stress for the team. Like any other startup, there were relationships to manage from employees to investors. There was years' worth of hard work on the line and they needed to keep going.

It was at this moment, when everything in my life was burning, that I saw a *glimpse*. Akin to my brother's glimpse in South Africa, I saw something different for the first time.

Before this moment, I had moved through life using intelligence and willpower. I worked very, very hard to escape my demons. I came from an abusive and dysfunctional environment, the byproduct of a family member whose trauma and hurt went unprocessed. However, there was a key difference between my experience and theirs: I had the privilege (and eventually opportunity) to access mental health support, while they did not

I felt so alone at that moment, grieving Keane's death. Who else could understand what I had survived and what I was going through?

In that moment of rock bottom, of finding a way to survive, my glimpse whispered, "This can't be true. You're not alone. Surely, there must be others like you."

Four weeks after the funeral, I delved into this glimpse. Tactical and lean like a founder, I emailed 50 tech founders and asked if I could sit down with them one-on-one. I wanted to know:

1. What was it *really* like for them, being a founder?
2. Was I the only one who lived through this kind of pain? Was I alone in my experience?
3. When they look back at their business failures, what was the number one reason why they failed?

I was a ball of nerves. Tender and exposed, I had never asked my peers these questions before. Before this moment, our conversations were safe and even predictable: fundraising, legal, and operations. This, right here, was a different ball game.

It was real talk.

The conversations I had over the next several months blew me away.

The more I sat with the founders, the more I heard something. Something small, subtle, and repeating, especially around their business failures:

- "I knew my co-founder wasn't the right person to scale this company. I should have asked them to leave. I waited until the last possible moment to talk to them."
- "We were running out of cash flow and I didn't want to admit it. I waited until our company went nearly bankrupt to ask for help from my investors."
- "I was burnt out. I was so good at what I did, but I hated my life. I was so embarrassed to admit that I didn't want to be the CEO of my company anymore."

In the glimpse, the pattern I saw was *avoidance*. Thirty-five of the 50 founders (70%) cited avoidance as the number one reason for their business failures. People were holding on to their secrets and masks and they were hurting themselves, their families, and their companies. Highly successful people, hiding in plain sight, not allowing themselves or anyone else to see what was real.

And what was more remarkable?

We had so many of these founder stories intertwined with mental health and trauma that there were more survivors (people with direct experience) than allies. Despite their large and affluent networks, they had been hiding for long periods of time. I had people in hiding for six years, all the way to three decades.

That's a long time, pretending to be someone you're not.

THE SECOND PANDEMIC

This book has gone through hell and back. I meant to release this book in the fall of 2023, and six weeks before the finished books arrived at my house my former publisher became insolvent. It was shocking and sudden and it hurt.

It hurt to be so close to the finish line and to feel the opportunity, the opportunity to impact thousands or even millions of people, to be taken away from us. That after 2.5 years of tolling away to bring this book to you, I had another marathon ahead of me.

I share this part of my story because I am grateful to my publisher, Wiley, for taking the leap with me. We spent eight months talking behind closed doors to see whether or not this book, a book that is essentially about the importance of tough conversations, was a good partnership for both of us. In discussing with my Executive Editor Bill Falloon (thank you, Bill!), we came to the mutual conclusion that this book was and is needed more than ever on the planet.

The fact is, every organization and every workplace in the world is going through what I call a **second pandemic** – not a physical one, but a mental health one. Every entrepreneur, leader, and organization out there is faced with the threat of their survival as a business, in the face of the most massive and systemic problems of our lifetime, from climate change to artificial intelligence.

For far too long, leaders have risen to this challenge by doing more. Working harder. And asking their direct reports, their employees, to do the same. But people are tired and are fed up. Every day, I check Reddit for the latest news to get a pulse of how people are thinking and really feeling – and it's not good. New subreddits like r/antiwork and r/canadahousing convey a sentiment where the American dream is broken and even nonexistent: no longer can the security and success we dream of be achieved through hard work. Working as hard as you can, for as long as you can, is no longer an acceptable solution for my generation and the generations to come.

The reality is that hard work is no longer enough to survive and succeed. We need to work smarter, not harder, in order to stay relevant and valuable to the people we serve, and we do this by innovating. By creating products or services, often utilizing the latest technologies, in order to win the game of innovation.

Every leader and every organization must innovate, not just entrepreneurs.

When I started as an entrepreneur nearly two decades ago, it was fringe and counterculture to be an entrepreneur, much less one in the tech space. I remember taking computer classes in high school (encouraged by my dad) and being the only girl in my Computer Engineering class. I was learning how to code with Python and they had just introduced typing classes at school, where we were given keyboard devices for the purposes of learning how to type.

When I wrote this book with my previous publisher, I initially imagined this as a survival guide for tech founders, having worked with so many of them as clients or as colleagues for decades. I had seen the necessity of #REALTALK, where tech founders were going through unnatural and immense work pressures that are destabilizing on a daily basis, from being sued to having your whole business model become irrelevant the next day.

Now, as I imagine the people reading this book, this manifesto is for the tech founders *and* for the leaders of the future. My mission is to see *every leader build the future of their organization, without burning out.* I want a world where every leader feels good and even empowered to come into work each day, ready to meet the challenges that innovation and technology have set for us, because they have the mindset, heartset, and skillset to meet their circumstances head-on as a leader.

How will you meet the circumstances of tomorrow? Who is the leader that you can become?

CHAPTER TWO

BRAVE NEW WORLD

It was January 2018 and every day felt like sink or swim.

Traditionally, every New Year was marked by a new energy, a space to breathe and to create. It was a time to let go of the past and embrace all that was to come. There was something about the freshness of winter, paired with the first day of a new year, that brought out a feeling of curiosity and anticipation in me.

This year felt different.

There was certainly newness in my life, but it was jarring. It felt like the thrashing of an ocean, the waves were 30-feet high and crashing down on all the things I knew about life and washing them away. What could survive against a force of nature such as this?

As a sister and as a daughter, all I wanted more than anything in those days was for things to stay. For the memories, the companies, and the life that I built with Keane to remain permanent – as if nothing could take them away. It was unrealistic and it was desperate, but the feelings were real. I felt like a little girl again, taking my tiny hands and trying to protect my creations, knowing deep down that they were impermanent under the force of change.

Even this one.

In the face of my 30-foot wave, it was a *brave new world*. Like the 1932 book of the same name by Aldous Huxley, I was faced with such a circumstance: a long future where life felt meaningless. Instead of an abundant future for all, powered by technology and money like the work that Keane and I shared through one decade of entrepreneurship, the world became bleak. It became hard, cold, and unfeeling.

I had never imagined a future where I would be on the other side, celebrating the successes that Keane and I dreamed of as kids, only to have an empty space by my side. I was learning that no amount of money or success could replace the loss I experienced.

I would trade any amount of money or success if it meant I could have Keane back.

At such a turning point in my life, all these problems were coming to a head. It was time to act; everything I built would either thrive or die based on the decisions I made. Could I show up for myself, my family, and my community before it was too late?

How was I going to show up as a leader? What was the world I wanted to create with others?

A NECESSARY CONDITION OF LEADERSHIP

As a faculty member at the Schulich School of Business, one of Canada's preeminent schools, I shape the next generation of leaders: eager fourth-year undergrads and second-year MBAs who are discovering entrepreneurship for the first time. I teach three Entrepreneurship courses at the school, but my favorite one is called Social Entrepreneurship. Every year, my class and I take a field trip to the Centre for Social Innovation. It is Canada's largest social innovation community, the home to over 3000 social enterprises from every vertical imaginable.

One year, my students had a chance to meet Tonya Surman, its founder and CEO. She has been building social ventures since the 1980s, back when it was early and even unpopular. I will never forget that moment, sitting in the room, when one of my students stood up and asked, "I watch the news and what's happening in the world, and it's hard not to get depressed. Everything is going wrong and the odds are stacked against us. How do you push on when you don't want to?"

He was 22 years young and just starting his journey into the workplace. What a heaviness to bear.

As leaders of leaders, whether you are a tech founder or a manager at a company, our leadership matters. The way we show up matters. It is a daily choice to lead in these times and to engage with reality. To acknowledge the state of the world, along with systemic inequalities like gender and race. For too long, leaders have turned a blind eye to the tough conversations, denying their existence or even perpetuating harm.

To be involved with and aware of what's real, the *real* in #REALTALK is a **necessary condition of leadership**. You cannot solve something that you are not willing to see or talk about. Period.

Employees are no longer tolerating the abuses and the overwork that have occurred in the workplace for decades. Especially in these times, coming from a pandemic into a recession and the options made available by remote work, employees no longer feel loyal to the companies they serve . . . unless they are led by a leader who cares, who inspires, and who shows up with high levels of integrity and also performance.

Subpar conditions will no longer cut it, and the importance of utilizing real talk in our everyday interactions has mattered and matters more than ever, given the magnitude of the problems the world is facing today.

Historically, workplaces have not been the bastions of real talk—quite the opposite. For decades, employees have feared retaliation from their bosses and/or peers if they were to show any kind of human vulnerability. To understand how workplaces got to this point, we need to understand the human brain. As humans, we do poorly at seeing and understanding things as they occur. This pattern is the foundation of the work of Dr Daniel Kahneman, one of the most influential psychologists of our time. In his *New York Times* best-selling book *Thinking Fast and Slow*, Kahneman reports the phenomenon called **cognitive biases**: faulty ways of thinking that affect our daily decision-making.[1]

Here are the most relevant cognitive biases affecting leaders today:

Attribute Substitution

Attribution substitution occurs when we take a complex problem and replace it with a simpler and incorrect interpretation. This thinking can be dangerous, causing leaders to miss key information or variables. For example, attribute substitution is occurring in the conversation on race. In the tech industry, where most executives are White men, many people believe that Black Lives Matter is similar to the Women in Tech movement.

It is an oversimplification since Black people have been disproportionately affected by generational trauma, physical violence, and systems of power. This bias does not allow for more nuanced considerations, such as individuals who are from two or more underrepresented communities. In mental health, we call this **intersectionality**: an individual is impacted by a combination of discrimination and disadvantages, which must be taken into account.

Availability Heuristic

The availability heuristic occurs when people use immediate examples, especially from their own lives, to evaluate a topic, concept, or decision.

They assume the easier we can recall an idea, the more likely the event. For example, Left-leaning Americans and international readers were surprised by the 2020 US elections. Many individuals and media outlets assumed that the Right would lose by a landslide.

Despite President Biden winning the election, former President Trump received 46.9% of the popular vote, meaning that 74 million Americans supported him for a second term. Former President Trump has a devoted base of supporters, which the Left has miscalculated because they surround themselves with people who think like them. It is this mistake that cost the Democrats the 2016 elections with Hillary Clinton, in ignoring the growing support and dialog of the Right.

Hindsight Bias

Hindsight bias occurs when people label the cause of an event as *obvious* after that event has happened. Humans are often poor predictors of events, as seen in quantitative data and longitudinal studies, where participants in experiments are tracked over decades. For example, Future of Work experts claim that the widespread adoption of work-from-home was inevitable. However, it was not until COVID-19 that there was a tipping point for action.

Despite technology like Zoom, which has existed since 2012, it took the closing of nonessential services and the enforcement of government-mandated lockdowns for companies to implement remote work. In older industries, such as finance, legal, and retail, there continues to be disagreement around work-from-home practices post-pandemic. Different industries and different generations have their own definitions of productivity, where productivity was once "doing your time" at the office.

Given these cognitive biases, which are hardwired into our brains, what does it all mean?

Choosing to be real, to lead from reality rather than the preferences we hold, requires intention. It requires practice. Like building muscle, we must exercise our ability to see problems for what they are so that we can better serve our people. By doing so, we can be more responsive in the workplace by addressing problems as they occur, and having the necessary conversations with ourselves, our teams, and our organizations to solve them.

Our world depends on it.

THE GAME OF INNOVATION

In starting this chapter, I want you to remember that thriving and innovating are not short-term games. They are long-term games. They need to be long-term games because in my personal and professional spaces, I have seen what has happened when we pursue success by paying too high of a cost. We lose ourselves, and eventually, we lose our teams, our companies, and even our families because we no longer become the leader that is needed to rise to the occasion.

In my career, I have had the privilege of working with the most successful people on the planet, particularly tech founders who have built and sold the most innovative companies in our lifetime. I talk about tech founders often in this book because it is from their example that I train my corporate clients, many of whom are entering the game of innovation for the first time. The mistakes and victories of tech founders can teach you what is truly necessary to birth new, groundbreaking companies with little resources or under significant duress.

Tech founders and the asset class associated with them (venture capital) have been here since the 1940s, and they know how to play the game of innovation and to win. I share this context because since starting #REALTALK all those years ago, our work has evolved and impacted me in ways I didn't expect.

When I lost my brother Keane, I used to think that #REALTALK and the immense stresses we were trying to solve were just for tech founders. Things like depression, anxiety, burnout, and even change fatigue. However, as our work continues to spread, what I have realized time and time again is that *all companies are or will be tech companies.* Every company from a startup all the way to a conglomerate must adopt the latest technologies, especially artificial intelligence and the metaverse, because their customers demand it.

In venture capital (VC), there are said and unsaid rules should you choose to enter the game of innovation. One of the golden rules of VC is that if you are going to raise money (we call it a "fundraising tour"), you need to acquire, execute, and iterate without stopping. Once you have declared in the innovation ecosystem that you are raising funds, eyes are on you and your startup's performance.

There is a psychological factor to innovation too, where proposing innovation seems uncertain and even contradictory at first. According to famed investor Howard Marks, winning the game of innovation requires an organization to be both non-consensus *and* right, meaning that being a first mover matters (even when it seems crazy) and that the prediction or investment made must be right.[2] If we become consensus or wrong, just one of the two, we lose a significant amount of the high-risk, high-reward that makes the game of innovation worth it to begin with.

In navigating a brave new world, what I call the "game of innovation," corporations must learn how to plan extensively and to commit. Once our ship has started its sail across the waters of innovation, it means adapting as individuals and as a collective to get to the other side. If we try a half-hearted attempt while we are in the water, our ship will sink or worse: we will have ruined the credibility and morale of our crew, making it unlikely for future attempts at innovation to succeed.

WHAT WE CAN LEARN FROM VENTURE CAPITAL

In the last few years, I have had the privilege of being on the other side of the table, where I was General Partner of an early-stage VC firm called

Renew Venture Capital. I made this career transition, after months of deliberate thinking, because I admired their work and their mission.

Venture capital is a worldwide asset class that has produced some of the highest amounts of innovation. There are household apps that you cannot imagine your life without, from Uber to Airbnb, which were birthed from this sector. These startups have faced immense pressures to innovate, survive, and thrive and because of these pressures, they have developed best practices of what it really takes to bring innovation to life. Not as a concept, not as a strategy, but as a true-and-tried product or service used by millions (and sometimes billions) of people on the planet.

Why learn from venture capital? Since the birth of this small but mighty asset class, venture capital has garnered a reputation for punching above its weight. Venture capital is a subset of private equity, where stakeholders like high-net-worth individuals, family offices, funds of funds, and more invest into venture capital funds in the hopes of an "outsized return." These body of stakeholders are called **limited partners (LPs)**, where an outsized return is 3–5× of the principal, the initial amount invested. Unlike other types of investment, such as stocks, once an investment is made into a startup, the money is considered to be "illiquid." It means waiting many years (sometimes as long as a decade) before knowing the true result of your investment: loss, break even, or win. It has major implications for LPs because startups face so many stressful and even unexpected problems from hiring to patenting to go-to-market strategy. **Venture capitalists (VCs)** act as asset managers of this money, where their responsibility is to help the startups survive, to increase the value of the startups themselves, and to eventually sell or liquidate those startups, in order to return the principal and a fat chunk of profit to their LPs.

Thus, there is a never-ending pressure for venture-backed startups to not just be good or great, but best in class. World-changing. Market-defining. They need to be so good (think of a home run) that they can become a **unicorn**, a company worth at least $1 billion, in order to make the high risk and illiquidity worth it.

After all, if venture capital isn't giving us an outsized return, why not just invest my money into stocks or real estate or mutual funds? Why not just skip venture capital altogether?

VCs are aware that the game of innovation is and has always been a long-term, high-stakes game. There is no option for short term, not one that would create the tangible and intangible benefits that shareholders would want to see, in order to have enduring success in the market. Not only that, since VCs have played the game of innovation since its inception, they understand the gravity of the situation: the true length of time required to make innovation happen (often several years to a decade), plus the leadership skills necessary to make this a reality.

When I think of the profound pressures of this "game," I both admire and fear it. Even in the early days of venture capital, when it emerged in the 1940s, its ethos was about adapting and pivoting long enough to thrive. To survive and thrive past every competitor and every obstacle along the decade-long journey.

The VC asset class was initially created to fund businesses that were illegible for bank loans or government funding. These businesses were considered to be "too risky" because they broke the traditional mold: being unable to show metrics like revenue or customers to qualify for a loan. In the world of startups, we call this **pre-revenue**, where the innovation or product is still in development. Truly innovative products, ones that are world-changing and market-defining, can take years to develop before they enter the mainstream market. They have a unique commercialization cycle that is different from traditional businesses.

In understanding what VC and startups have meant to me and the world, this book will cover best practices drawn from my real-world experiences as a fifth-generation entrepreneur, tech founder, and venture capitalist. My family has been building companies for 140 years, and in looking at the 40 000 tech leaders I have coached or trained through #REALTALK, you can build the muscle and the leadership skills necessary to build the future of your organization, while staying sane, healthy, and happy in the long term.

Furthermore, venture capital has been known to punch above its weight, a dynamic that more organizations big and small will want to tap into. With rising costs and job cuts, even the largest of companies (where many of my speaking clients come from) are desiring to run lean rather than at excess. They want to innovate, but to maximize the output and the results created from their financial and human investment.

For instance, economic professor Ilya A. Strebulaev at the Stanford Graduate School of Business published a paper in 2015, quantifying the long-term impact of VC on the American economy.[3] He found that industries like food, retail, and biotech have been catalyzed by venture capital, with household names like Apple, Google, Amazon, Tesla, Whole Foods, Starbucks, and Costco being backed by VCs in its earlier days, when each of these companies was considered to be an innovative player in its industry.

However, what is even more startling is that over the past 50 years, US venture capital has raised $0.6 trillion to invest, while US private equity has raised four times the size. Given its small size as an asset class, VC-backed companies truly punch above their weight by accounting for the following in the United States since 1979:

- Forty-three percent of all public companies
- Fifty-seven percent of total market capitalization
- Thirty-eight percent of total employees
- Eighty-two percent of research and development

Thus, looking at the best practices of the startup world can help us understand how to thrive and innovate in these changing times.

THE URGENT NEED FOR REALNESS

This book exists because after working with over 40 000 leaders, our team at #REALTALK hit a plateau. We were traveling to conferences and organizations around the world, but we were failing. Failing to bring real talk to an entire industry in a more permanent way. Despite the life-changing moments our clients experienced, the mental health crisis was growing faster than we could deliver its solution.

Our in-person process wasn't enough for the tech industry. Not anymore.

It has taken a significant investment of time and money for this book to exist in your hands. At #REALTALK, we believe that the time for real talk is now. It must be **now**.

In the last decade, there have been key studies done on the impact of avoiding difficult or uncomfortable conversations (what we call "real talk") in the workplace. There has been a distinct lack of courage and leadership at work, in stepping up to voice concerns and to handle confrontations. In a 2017 survey by Quantum Workplace and Fierce Conversations, 53% of employees handled toxic situations by ignoring or avoiding them and only 24% addressed those situations directly.[4] Furthermore, more than 40% of employees believe that their leaders do nothing once the problem has been reported, and only 20% of employees believe their colleague would change if confronted.

There is an underlying reason for the lack of tough conversations in our leaders, our teams, and our organizations. I believe every person, regardless of their rank or title, is a leader in their own right: they must lead themselves and others. The way they show up affects an entire organization for better or for worse. To emphasize the importance of seeing ourselves this way, I call these individuals **leaders of leaders:** people who have internal and/or external stakeholders who depend on them (e.g. direct reports, new clients, existing vendors) and whose example has ripple effects in their workplace. Depending on how they react or respond, their example can either create a resilient workplace that embraces tough conversations or a fragile one whose grievances veer the organization toward a point of no return.

This book was written for leaders of leaders, to help them reclaim their leadership and their power in the workplace and in life. When leaders of leaders are unable to exemplify these traits and the workplace continues to be an unsafe place, it directly affects organizational morale, productivity, and collaboration. In being unable to acknowledge these situations or challenges immediately and when they are still small, many of them snowball and create secondary feelings of resentment, frustration, or even helplessness.

I saw this pattern regularly in the tech founders and leaders we worked with at #REALTALK, and this pattern has notable consequences for every level of the organization. Leadership training company VitalSmarts conducted a 2016 study of 1025 people in the US workforce and found the following:[5]

- Seventy-two percent reported a failure to address a colleague who was slacking off
- Sixty-eight percent reported a failure to address disrespect
- Fifty-seven percent have witnessed peers skip important workplace processes
- Forty percent have wasted two or more weeks ruminating about a breakdown in conversation
- The cost of avoidance (per conversation) was an average of $7500 in lost time and resources

The need for realness is not just for morale or to do good but is essential in keeping an effective workplace operating. Bravely, a coaching and training platform for employees, published a white paper on what they call the "conversation gap," where employees stop communicating with one another.[6] Similar to what I found in my #REALTALK interviews with 50 tech CEOs, Bravely found that 70% of workers avoid difficult conversations with their boss, colleagues, or direct reports. This number is similar to our 70% finding that the number one reason for business failure has been conversational avoidance from tech founders.

Being real and having these tough conversations is no longer a nice-to-have. It is an essential skill all leaders must embody to address everyday concerns, to build psychological safety, and to create a workplace that actually empowers people to thrive and innovate in modern times.

THE RISE OF MICROCOMMUNITIES

Trend Hunter is the largest trends and innovation database in the world, with extensive reports on the upcoming trends in every industry. During COVID-19, they released a special report called *The New Normal*. One of the trends listed was **tribalism**, the concept that humans self-organize into smaller communities to satisfy their need for belonging. We are already seeing tribalism occur, in a political, economic, and technological backdrop where many employees are unhappy at work. In a workplace where people aren't talking to one another, trust erodes and anxiety increases. Employees may be thinking to themselves, *Who do I trust? Why am I still working with this person? Why don't I just leave?*

As remote work and physical isolation increase, the loneliness crisis will worsen as well. I see it in my young students and entrepreneurs, who feel much older than they are. In a world of infinite choices, where we can self-select our "tribes" (known as **community**), people want to find and be with their own – specific and intersectional, embodying all the identities that create belonging.

The need for belonging is innate, unconscious, and powerful. It cannot be reasoned away and represents thousands of years of biological patterning. Our ancestors gathered in physical communities to survive and to have enough food, shelter, and protection in groups. Having a community that you belong to is not just for physical safety, but it's for our long-term sanity and happiness as well. With longer work hours and less purchasing power, many of us feel that working hard and doing our best is no longer the pathway to a meaningful or fulfilling life. In these painful circumstances, humans seek others for company, comfort, and understanding.

In these circumstances where our very survival has become ever-present, humans are not meant to be lone wolves. In desiring to find their community, people look to realness.

A dear friend of mine named Yanik Silver sees the same thing. The CEO of Maverick1000, one of the most impact-focused entrepreneurial communities in the world, he previously served on the Constellation Board for Virgin Unite, the charitable arm of Sir Richard Branson's Virgin Group. In his report *20 Predictions for the 2020s*, Silver notes that people seek curated community, a connection and joy felt from finding "your people."

You can only find your people when your people are sharing and being real. You cannot find something you cannot see. More importantly, your people cannot find you either, if you are hiding and pretending in everyday life.

Why does this trend matter, you ask? Why should I care?

While the world's problems are more widespread (systemic), they are also becoming more specific. Problems have become more specific because within a system, there are stakeholders who represent different intersections and needs in race, gender, economic status, and more. Since the pandemic, the need for specificity is not just a nice-to-have, but a make-or-break factor in high-stakes conversations on the national or global stage. When people have been let down by their institutions repeatedly, which includes the workplace, they begin to mistrust those systems, the leaders, and their policies.

For instance, the topic of housing and immigration has become a hot button issue in Canada. I have lived here for decades and many Canadians feel their concerns on affordable housing and groceries are being unheard or unaddressed by the government. As a result, a systemwide resentment and mistrust has occurred where Canadians have become critical of the influx of international students, the misuse of food banks, and the lack of policy changes in managing immigration numbers. Canadians are angry and cannot afford to live in the cities they have belonged to for so long.

In the face of drowning and despair, what our people want is to be seen and to be heard by their leaders and their peers. To know that we understand them and their concerns and that we will create solutions that help their specific group or community.

Without the foundation of real talk, the people we want to reach will continue to mistrust. To lash out (and perhaps, rightly so) because they feel the people at the top "don't get them" or even worse, "don't care." Without a bridge to talk with these individuals, we cannot create meaningful solutions to the problems we want to solve.

We need real talk to lower these walls and to start those conversations.

This observation is weaved throughout our work at #REALTALK. We quickly entered the market because our approach was based on community. In working with clients, we traveled to their communities rather than having communities travel to us. This approach was distinctive and refreshing, based on my previous life as an award-winning special education teacher. In working with highly vulnerable populations (students who experienced mental illness and abuse), I saw the resistance in talking about topics that seemed risky or vulnerable, such as their own mental health. I also learned through my two degrees in social and developmental psychology that if you are a leader who is bringing a conversation in the open, it is not just about breaking down walls, but a standard of care.

If people let their walls down, it is your responsibility to get them to an acceptable and satisfying conclusion. Building the bridge and tearing down walls only to disappoint them further with inaction or even continued harm could burn that bridge down for good. This lesson is especially important when reaching out to individuals from vulnerable or underserved communities, such as women or visible minorities, who have a history of being overlooked or dismissed at a systemic level.

Thus, in being in those classrooms with my special education students, I discovered that people had to be brought in. They had to agree. They had to say *yes* for the conversation to start and to have a meaningful voice in that conversation, in order to keep going.

This realization is why #REALTALK has traveled to communities and continues to inform my practice as an innovation and mental health speaker as well. The most effective leadership is when the members of those communities participate and own the solutions being created. We have traveled to tech accelerators, conferences, and hubs, launching #REALTALK Circles *with* their community leaders. I have traveled to corporations, associations, and universities too, translating and bringing these lessons of thriving and innovating to workplaces around the world.

In all of these instances, my role as a leader of leaders is not talking *at* them or *to* them, but *with* them. Working as partners.

Similar to our work at #REALTALK, this book is doing the same thing. This book is traveling to you, the leader of leaders, so that you may create real talk in your own community. Your community can be your family, your team, or even your organization. By having real talk exist in your spaces or your communities, regardless of whether or not we are physically there at the time – that becomes true power.

That is the power to build the bridge. That is the power to transform an industry. That is the power to solve the mental health crisis and to win the game of innovation, which has affected the lives of the colleagues, friends, and family that we hold dear.

A WORLD THAT WORKS FOR HUMANITY

In the 1950s, there was a renowned architect, futurist, and inventor named Buckminster Fuller. He was one of the first futurists in the world, perhaps best known for inventing the geodesic dome, like the Epcot dome in Walt Disney World, Florida.

Fuller took on problems of a global, systemic scale like transportation, energy, and housing. He got into the ring and gathered other leaders to his stand. He led when no one else wanted to. He allowed himself to get curious and to listen compassionately, to understand the problems of other people. It was Fuller who famously said, "Make the world work, for 100 percent of humanity, in the shortest possible time, through spontaneous cooperation, without ecological offense or the disadvantage of anyone."

Like Fuller, we as tech founders and leaders of leaders are this century's futurists, searching for ways to make the world work for everyone, but we have to start with our own community.

In the tech industry, we have made some progress on issues like racism and sexism, but we have a long way to go. Despite the $83 billion invested by VCs each year and the billions that VCs stand to lose from underperforming founders, #REALTALK was a hard movement to build. Very hard.

When we first started, I spent eight months educating founders and investors on mental health. Despite a 72% mental illness rate for entrepreneurs, tech leaders were in denial. Instead of a willingness to acknowledge the problem – to be real – founders thought themselves invincible. It was common to be in circles with my peers and to hear of another founder struggling with burnout, depression, or addiction.

By the time we ended our first year, I knew of 10 tech founders or investors who completed suicide – leaders from other cities, whose friends or family reached out to #REALTALK privately. Mind you, this was before COVID-19 and the recession that followed, so I imagine these numbers would be higher now.

They wanted us to know one thing: that our work mattered – that we had to keep going.

Despite the supposed power of being founders, we have often been bystanders. Apathetic. Allowing our people to suffer and die.

Many years have passed since the birth of #REALTALK, and what has been most concerning is the bystanding and enabling that continues to exist. #REALTALK works with leaders of leaders and their mental health, and for many years we were one of the only players in this space. I know it to be true because we received thousands of messages from tech founders, investors, and even media who told us so.

It wasn't until COVID-19 ravaged the planet that other organizations stepped up, working alongside us in the name of Founder Mental Health. Since then, we have experienced a fourth evolution in our work at #REALTALK, where leaders of leaders from all walks of life (not just tech founders) are drawn to the lessons and strategies of this book.

The fact is that real conversations are hard to find and even harder to sustain, but that is where solutions start. The solutions we need in the workplace and in our lives have to not just create short-term impact, but long-term impact. People are tired, frustrated, and lacking capacity, and they need a path forward that feels stable and trustworthy as we build together.

We need to have conversations in the open and with each other, for systemwide transformation to occur. In the game of business and innovation, these conversations are often emotionally charged because the stakes are so high. Are we pivoting our entire business model? Are we laying off 15% of our staff? Are we entering a new market or country, or staying where we are? Will we integrate artificial intelligence like our competitors?

It is these questions and the climbing pressures of the workplace that motivate so many employees to seek out leaders and workplaces that are doing good. That are leading the charge, rather than waiting for catastrophe to engage in real talk. Without rising to the occasion and our standards as leaders, we become prey to our circumstances.

A dysfunctional status quo that diminishes the humanity and potential that lives in all of us.

THE CALL TO COURAGE

In picking up this book, my invitation to you is to make the choice. To make the conscious decision to do this work and to follow through. It has been the craziest journey getting this book into existence and sometimes,

I have to laugh. I went through a car accident, my brother's passing, my mother's late-stage cancer, my dad's late-stage cancer, and the dissolving of my previous publisher in order to bring this book to you.

In a poetic sort of way, when I thought I was done with this book, this book wasn't done with me. I would be confronted with another complex and difficult situation to resolve, an invitation to revisit and reinforce the many lessons, frameworks, and strategies I will share with you.

A call to courage that asked me, as a leader of leaders, to embody this work in a deeper way.

Writing this book and even sharing pieces of its work through keynotes with clients, backroom conversations, and more has been the most transformational and yet difficult of journeys. I have laughed and cried in experiencing these lessons again and again, and in initiating (and completing) tough conversations in my own life.

However, I will say this: I have no regrets. Every day, I am grateful for the events and this body of work because I am stronger, more resilient, and more generous than ever before. The me of 10 years ago, even the me of 5 years ago, would have never fathomed a version of Cherry Rose Tan that could withstand the multiple tsunamis that came my way, plus the increased responsibilities I chose to take on. The me of before could never imagine co-founding a VC firm or running a national ecosystem of 250 startups, under the crucible and weight of such hardship.

The reality is that every single one of us has struggled. If it wasn't the pandemic, then it was the recession. If it wasn't a recession, maybe it was a personal or professional loss you experienced. Or maybe it was good ol' life that gave you a curveball.

Regardless of what brought you here to this book, I welcome you into this conversation and this journey. This journey will demand of you your best, and it will push you to uncover your demons and to resolve them so that you can be the leader of leaders who wakes up each day and goes to bed with peace of mind and an unshakeable fortitude in your work.

UNDERSTANDING THE THREE CONVERSATIONS

Still Standing is a field guide on having tough and real conversations as a founder. **Real talk is a necessary condition of leadership**; it is the key behind our work with over 40 000 leaders and how we have made strides in solving the crisis on workplace mental health. It is the key behind the work I now do with corporations, associations, and universities across the globe, who need a pathway to thriving and innovating under incredible pressure.

By the end of this book, you will have a step-by-step, ready-to-use system for applying real talk in all areas of your life, especially your work.

To master the essential skill of real talk, this book splits into three **Conversations:**

Conversation	Chapter	Focus
#REALTALK with Me	Stability	Mind (Thoughts)
	Integrity	
	Workability	
#REALTALK with You	Awareness	Heart (Emotions)
	Compassion	
	Forgiveness	
#REALTALK with Us	Identity	Will (Actions)
	Reclamation	
	Sovereignty	

The exercises, research, and resources provided in each chapter will enable you to integrate your newfound knowledge and apply it to your daily life. This book can help you, your team, and your organization **unlock the three conversations that can mean the difference between thriving**

and dying: mentally, emotionally, and even financially. In embodying real talk in your workplace (and eventually, other areas of life), you will unlock a level of leadership capacity that will allow you to innovate and win in the face of uncertainty.

In every workplace, we cannot help or support each other until we take the *first step*. We need to start by admitting we have a problem, that our circumstances aren't working for us, and having a conversation about it.

That is real talk.

I have sat with the most successful founders and CEOs in the world and I have seen it all: depression, anxiety, addiction, grief, domestic violence, and more, combined with the stresses of running teams, companies, and even empires. As you embark on this book and lean into *real* conversations, remember what you are fighting for.

We are fighting for a world where leaders are supported by their own. A brave new world.

PART I

THE FIRST CONVERSATION

#REALTALK with Me

The first part, or Conversation, is about having real conversations with **yourself**. In working with tech founders and leaders of leaders, I have noticed a discernible pattern when it comes to mental health and real conversations. Rather than leaning into the conversation, many leaders avoid or deny it. Our 1300 pages of qualitative data have revealed that if leaders lack integrity with themselves, such as living in pretend, it becomes difficult (and sometimes unbearable) to lead themselves, their teams, and their organizations.

This Conversation with yourself addresses the **Mind (Thoughts).** As leaders, we can strengthen our mindset toward personal and professional challenges, rather than suppressing or running away from those thoughts. I have sat with hundreds of tech CEOs who have been hiding their humanity for *decades*, unable or unwilling to ask for support. This martyrdom is filled with drama, pressure, and sacrifice rather than acknowledging that the game of business and innovation is messy and that we aren't alone.

Being real with yourself is essential because it creates the necessary conditions for responsible leadership: acknowledging mistakes and fixing them as soon as possible. All organizational change starts from this place because without buy-in from the stakeholders with the most power, meaningful change can never occur company-wide. When leaders care more about **being right instead of real**, they lose the ability to adapt. They can no longer hear, see, or speak from reality.

CHAPTER THREE

STABILITY

It was February 2018 and the walls were closing in.

Everywhere I looked and everywhere I went, I saw chaos. It was two months since my brother's passing and I was distraught. On top of that, I was facing the mortality of my mum, who was battling Stage 3C endometrial cancer. She had ended up at one of the largest cancer treatment centers in North America.

I remember the day we sat with my mother, waiting for her to undergo surgery. She was nervous, exhausted, and grieving for Keane, but it was necessary. The doctors needed to remove as much of the cancer growth as possible before it was too late.

Stage 3C was advanced. We were racing against the clock.

After her surgery, she was admitted to the Intensive Care Unit (ICU) for observation. The staff ran out of beds in the cancer ward and they moved her there. The doctors said her surgery was a success and they offered to send her home to recover. My dad and I said no; we wanted her to stay at the hospital. Keane's death felt sudden, untimely, and fresh and we didn't want to take chances.

We insisted that she stay overnight, despite her initial resistance. My mum hated being in the hospital. It reminded her too much of Keane and loss, but she agreed.

A few hours later, she began to feel nauseous and dizzy. The nausea got so bad that she felt like vomiting all the time – a terrible sign after a major surgery. Concerned, the doctors rushed to complete her bloodwork and found a concerning fact: her hemoglobin levels were less than half. This discovery was terrifying for someone like my mum, who had a lifelong history of anemia, a blood disorder where healthy red blood cells are low and clotting becomes difficult.

Her condition quickly became critical.

In the span of a few minutes, consent forms were signed and the staff opened an operating room for her. All the surgeons who were qualified to do this procedure were at home. The staff paged the surgeons in the middle of the night; they were driving and on the way.

We were so thankful (and lucky) that she survived those next 24 hours.

At the same time, my dad fainted. With the stress of my mum's condition against the fresh backdrop of Keane's death, he couldn't breathe. The nurses put him in a wheelchair and I was behind him, rolling him toward the emergency room. I wanted to stay with my mum, but she wanted me to stay with my dad.

It felt like everything was falling apart. What was I going to do?

WHY STABILITY MATTERS

Teaching at the Schulich School of Business, I host work-term students each year. These students request to work with me because they want to become social entrepreneurs. They are passionate about solving big problems, like climate change and affordable housing, and they want to learn from someone who has been there. Many of them are also drawn to the game of innovation, wanting a behind-the-scenes look at how founders operate some of the most innovative companies on the planet.

One thing that has surprised my students is the structure of my life. As the leader of a national ecosystem, I have a public persona. People see me on stage and in the media. Unlike other businesses, my work conversations delve into the mental and emotional, where I am often dealing with emotionally charged situations on a daily basis.

Founders come to me when they are struggling.

Due to the intensity of my work, stability matters. Foundation matters. I am all-in as a founder and as a leader of leaders *and* I treat self-care and recovery as seriously as my work meetings. I have structures in place for exercise, sleep, journaling, and more. I lead by example too; my team takes time off for vacation and we end every week with acknowledgments and wins.

Inspired by Olympic athletes, I treat myself as a valuable asset that requires maintenance and care. There is a plan, a system, a strategy in place to maintain my base levels of self-care (what I call "stability"), so that my body and my mind can withstand the multiple challenges that occur in my personal or professional life.

Unfortunately, the tech industry and workplaces in general encourage the opposite. Founders and leaders of leaders "hustle and grind" for 80–100 hours per week, wearing their burnout like a badge of honor. My late brother passed away in his sleep, after a prolonged lifestyle of working 120 hours per week.

It was only after he had passed that I discovered the extent of his workaholism. By then, it was too late. Why had no one stopped him?

In the workplace, we have become bystanders and enablers. We become desensitized to the real and grave implications of this do-whatever-it-takes culture and the effects it has on founders. In an iconic 2015 study by psychologist Dr. Michael Freeman, he discovered that entrepreneurs are 50% more likely to have a mental health condition and reported that:[1]

- Seventy-two percent have experienced mental illness
- Thirty percent have depression
- Twenty-seven percent have anxiety

Additionally, entrepreneurs are:

- Ten times more likely to have bipolar disorder
- Two times more likely to have suicidal thoughts
- Three times more likely to have an addiction

The crisis on workplace mental health has only increased since then. HubSpot conducted a 2022 study with hundreds of entrepreneurs and found that 63% are struggling with burnout, 59% are struggling with anxiety, and 47% are struggling with depression, a more than doubling of the anxiety rate since Freeman's research.[2] The same 2022 study also found that the top stressors of entrepreneurs (in order of priority) are financial concerns (21%), day-to-day stress (16%), and work-life balance (15%).

Thus, the problems in workplace mental health are tied with very specific stressors, many of them affecting our sense of psychological or financial safety. Leaders are working long hours and in a workplace culture that glorifies overwork, when in truth, the game of innovation is a long-term game where its players must endure a marathon, rather than a sprint.

On top of the mental health diagnoses discussed, our work at #REALTALK has identified patterns of addiction, workaholism, and divorce amongst tech founders and business leaders. Coming from the tech industry, I regularly heard of founders using harder substances like cocaine and heroin. Even though my background is mainly from the tech industry, I work with many clients (particularly corporations) in verticals like finance, law, and real estate, who can relate to these stories as well. Without healthy strategies, founders and leaders of leaders operate from empty, using whatever means or vices to get through the day.

Being lucky or reactive is not a strategy. Physical, mental, and emotional stability are critical to leaders of the future and a necessary condition for innovating and winning as organizations. Without stability for ourselves as leaders, how can we expect to lead others? How can we expect to lead from empty?

The fact is: It isn't possible or sustainable in the long run.

THE BIGGEST MISTAKE YOU CAN MAKE

Earlier in this book, I shared with you my belief that every company, every organization on this planet has been thrust into the game of innovation. No company can stay still without having their very existence threatened either in the short term or the long term because of the exponential technologies like AI, where your competitors are likely studying, strategizing, and looking to implement them to get ahead of you.

As a result, what leaders of leaders can learn from tech founders is the mistakes that are made when we build and scale too fast. Yes, that's right: What happens when we scale *too fast*.

When I was operating #REALTALK, the biggest mistake our tech founders made was the breakdown around self-care. Tech founders and leaders of leaders will start their careers or roles with a foundational level of self-care, the one they came in with. However, as they begin to take on progressively more tasks (and of higher difficulty), what will often occur is that their self-care practices erode. These leaders tell themselves that it's okay if they work some nights, then it becomes most nights, then it becomes weekends as well. As that pattern begins to build, their standards of self-care deteriorate quickly, until we tell ourselves that it's okay to compromise on our sleep, and then finally, to compromise on the time we take for our physical health and even our family.

The problem here is that stability and self-care become *more* important, not less important, when we scale in responsibility. As we scale our responsibilities, we need to scale our self-care (like the way that professional athletes do), so that we don't break down from the increased stress and workload.

It sounds like common sense (because it is), yet I rarely see tech founders and leaders of leaders do this well *and* for long periods of time.

Even in my life as a CEO, I have made the repeated mistake of pulling back on my self-care multiple times, only to pay the expensive cost (e.g., financial, physical, mental, social) in the future. It took several times to realize the importance of doubling down on self-care in order to stay a high performer in my industry.

When I was younger and starting my career, what self-care looked like to me was one-dimensional, such as eating healthy foods as I was working long hours (yes, I was guilty of the 80–100-hour work weeks too). However, as I have gotten older and as my responsibilities have grown, my layers of self-care have also increased. Now it means protecting my boundaries around sleep (I always get at least seven to eight hours of sleep), working out four times a week in high-intensity exercise, and meal planning on Sundays, so that my body is fueled with healthy foods during the week.

It is this intentional way I hold myself as a leader that has continued to be the foundation of my success. Furthermore, it trains self-discipline by mastering 0–1, not 0–100. Success comes from consistency and it means passing on short-term gratification in order to build and achieve the incredibly hard things. I speak of this concept regularly at my keynotes, where we are surrounded by media headlines that share misleading stories of success, of unicorn founders whose achievements appear overnight.

However, the fact is that before they got to their 100%, they started at 0–1. They started with the first building block or win they could handle and secured that, in order to build on top of that foundation. For instance, Shopify's CEO Tobias Lütke has been upfront about the importance of maintaining work-life balance, where he himself has never worked a night in the 18 years that Shopify has been in existence. Lütke and his co-founders have created an intentional culture that prevents employees from burnout, especially protecting nights and weekends, and invests in on-staff coaches to train their current and future leaders.[3]

By building the muscle of self-care, it will create a foundation of stability that you can fall back on during hard times. In talking with leaders of leaders who continue to find and maintain success for decades at a time, we have found that their journeys did not get easier. Instead, their leadership capacity to meet harder and more expensive challenges is what grew and made the difference. Case in point, there is a phenomenon in the startup industry where founders feel "they've made it" when they have raised a Series A or a Series B round (usually $10 million to $30 million). There is a false assumption that things are going to be "easier from here."

What becomes shocking to first-time founders is that it is the opposite: your responsibilities have significantly increased and the stakes are higher because you have investors watching. Now you report to a Board of Directors that has quantitative expectations on your performance, plus VC firms that are interested in growing the asset (your startup) at a rapid pace. A pace of building the plane as you're flying it. In some cases (especially after a Series B round), the head count of a startup doubles in a single year, which is a brutal pace for the inexperienced leader.

Thus, it's important we restore and strengthen our stability *now* and not when we are already in crisis, or when the stakes are too high. Remember that.

CREATING STABILITY IN THE JOURNEY

In this book, your journey is split into three parts or Conversations: with Me, with You, and with Us. Mastering real talk at each level is critical in creating organizations that thrive and innovate. Since founders and leaders of leaders will encounter incredible amounts of stress, we must build and weave stability early on, which starts in the mind.

As such, Chapters Three to Five are focused on the mastery of the mind, acknowledging that as leaders, we face a barrage of problems that can destabilize ourselves and our companies each day. We are navigating high-stakes decisions in product, hiring, and litigation, requiring critical thinking skills like analysis, synthesis, and visualization. However, when we are stuck in survival mode, our thoughts are focused on fear.

How do we restore our mental game?

In the coaching world, we use a concept called **distinction**. A distinction is a precise label of a situation, creating differences between words or concepts that appear to be the same thing (but aren't). When we are overwhelmed, our brain is overrun with cognitive biases, unable to see what is occurring in that situation. Like in the world of triage, there are two steps: the Diagnosis (the naming of the problem), followed by its Treatment (the solving of the problem).

By mislabeling a problem, solutions become less effective and in some cases, ineffective. The additional benefit of labeling things is that we soothe our overactive imaginations, where the anticipation of the supposed consequences can be just as stressful or more stressful than facing things head on.

The importance of distinctions is not just mental but biological. In developmental psychology, which is the study of cognitive development from birth to death, we learn that the human brain has three main areas:

1. The **prefrontal cortex** is the youngest part of the brain from an evolutionary standpoint. It handles higher-level functions like concentration, morality, and decision-making. Focused on cognitive, emotional, and behavioral functions, it is the source of our humanity.
2. The **hippocampus** is the middle child, neither the oldest nor the youngest part of the brain. It is responsible for learning and memory by forming, storing, and processing memories. Experiences like

flashbacks and re-experiencing of traumatic events come from this place.

3. The **amygdala** is the oldest part of our brain and is nicknamed the "reptilian brain." Vital to the hunter-and-gatherer days of humans, it detects fear and responds immediately. It creates the **fight-or-flight response**, a protective mechanism against danger.

Why does this matter? Humans mislabel situations and moments on a regular basis, unable to distinguish between fear and danger because of the immediate and reactive "reptilian brain." **Fear** is a reaction in the mind, anticipating a danger that has yet to be verified. On the other hand, **Danger** is a physical and immediate threat, preparing us to survive. It is the difference between a perceived threat like public speaking (Fear) versus a physical threat like spotting a wild bear (Danger).

The black-and-white nature of our reptilian brain is animalistic, primitive, and powerful. Prone to a negativity bias, humans devolve into fear easily, rather than reaching for possibility. This tendency has widespread implications when founders and leaders of leaders encounter high levels of uncertainty and change, like the times we are in.

Additionally, certain types of leaders may encounter these circumstances (and their impact on mental health) more than others. For example, many women in the tech industry have or currently experience microaggressions, sexual harassment, and stereotypes that they actively combat or avoid. Even in these emotionally charged situations, regardless of whether the behavior was intentional by the other party, it can trigger distressing sensations in the mind and body, which include fear.

The importance of having tools and strategies to navigate this fear is ever important. It is not about ignoring the fear or numbing the fear, but about building the muscle that allows us to approach each obstacle with a level of calmness or rationality, so that we have the opportunity to bring out our best selves in that situation.

#REALTALK LEADERSHIP

At #REALTALK, we have a model to describe the levels of performance available to founders. We call it **#REALTALK Leadership**. The success of each leader, their teams, and their organizations expands or shrinks, based on that leader's ability to have real conversations. We start with stability because as leaders, our performance sits in one of four levels:[4]

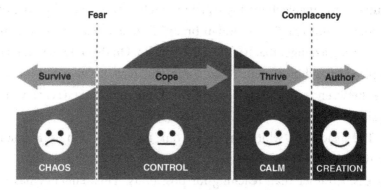

1. **Chaos:** At this level, leaders experience their world as **Chaos**. This state is the most reactive period of leadership, where conflict, drama, and breakdown appear in one or multiple areas of their lives. Chaos is problem-focused and urgent, activating the reptilian brain and leading to fear-based thinking. For leaders, their emotions are **detestable**, their conversations are **fake**, and their relationships are **harmful**. Leadership feels like a nonstop bombardment of problems with insufficient resources to address them, leading to quick-fix solutions. The primary action for the leader is **Survive** and **leadership is putting out fires**.

2. **Control:** At this level, leaders experience their world as **Control**. We have passed the line of Fear, so the organization has survived. However, the leader is incredibly busy, constantly micromanaging and risking burnout while working *in the business* (execution)

instead of *on the business* (strategy). For leaders, their emotions are **tolerable**, their conversations are **shallow**, and their relationships are **acceptable**. Unable to trust others, employees remain employees instead of leaders, causing the organization to thrive or die with that leader's individual performance. The primary action for the leader is **Cope** and **leadership is responding in the moment**.

3. **Calm:** At this level, leaders experience their world as **Calm**. The leader has breathing room. Financial and emotional needs are being met because team members have some agency, causing tasks to be delegated. For leaders, their emotions are **comfortable**, their conversations are **routine**, and their relationships are **meaningful**. The leader can work *on the business* (strategy) for the first time, directing and recruiting talent to build and operate the organization. The leader acts as the conductor of an orchestra rather than one of the musicians. The primary action for the leader is **Thrive** and **leadership is managing people and culture.**

4. **Creation:** At this level, leaders experience their world as **Creation**. It requires passing the line of Complacency, which represents the difference between "good enough" and excellence. By shifting from settling to possibility, the leader mobilizes their team to reveal blind spots and business opportunities. For leaders, their emotions are **valuable**, their conversations are **deep**, and their relationships are **profound**. Through communication (real talk), the leader can navigate any upset with poise, gathering different stakeholders for co-creation. Results can feel exponential and synchronous. The primary action for the leader is **Author**, and **leadership is building the shared future.**

To build on this concept of #REALTALK Leadership, it helps to understand the work of Abraham Maslow, an influential psychologist who studied human motivation.[5] He identified five categories of needs that dictate the behavior of all human beings, from the bottom of the hierarchy upwards: Physiological → Safety → Love & Belonging → Esteem → Self-Actualization. Humans are motivated to satisfy their lower-level needs first, such as physiological (e.g. water, food, shelter), before higher-level needs are considered.

We can apply Maslow's hierarchy of needs to the #REALTALK Leadership model, as founders and leaders of leaders will experience extreme highs and extreme lows as they navigate the game of innovation. The needs in these categories are fulfilled in chronological order from bottom to top, where our framework maps onto these naturally occurring human needs:

1. Physiological and Safety: **Chaos (Survive)**
2. Love and Belonging: **Control (Cope)**
3. Esteem: **Calm (Thrive)**
4. Self-Actualization: **Creation (Author)**

Similar to sports psychology, basic needs (e.g. nutrition, sleep) must be satisfied first; otherwise, it becomes difficult or even unhealthy to maintain our mental, emotional, or financial gains. Even the late Kobe Bryant, one of the best NBA players in history, worked with a sports psychologist and mindfulness teacher named George Mumford.[6] Rather than pushing himself to exhaustion and injury, Kobe shifted himself from survival to "the zone," known as **flow**. In an ABC interview, his teacher Mumford said, "You start talking to them about how the mind–body interacts . . . how you can slow time down when you create space between stimulus and response – [then] three seconds is an eternity."

As founders and leaders of leaders, we are the athletes, the superstars, the Olympians of the business world. We are the captains of our teams who have to perform and be "on" at a moment's notice.

You can't have a strong foundation without stability and having a strong foundation matters. Don't discount it!

QUESTIONS TO CREATE STABILITY

Stability is a state of mind, not a place to get to. When #REALTALK gets hired by leaders or organizations, they are usually heading toward crisis. As humans, we often wait until it is too late to act. That was my late brother's experience in an industry that encourages founders to work 100-hour weeks and waits until their founders are breaking down or dead to intervene.

Stability is a necessary first step because real talk is a muscle built through practice. When you invite real talk into your organization and your life, you get what you need, not what you want. For the unpracticed, it can be extremely triggering, leading to drama and upset. According to *Fortune Magazine*, 30% of startups fail because of the founder's emotional state: 13% from lost focus, 9% from lost passion, and 8% from founder burnout.[7]

There are three quick questions you can ask yourself to create stability. They can be used in the moment when you are overwhelmed and fearful:

What Is Really Happening?

How can I describe what I am experiencing as facts rather than as a narrative? It is natural for humans to create a narrative or story around an experience, bringing our biased interpretations and opinions about what happened. It takes practice to describe something *as it is*, without our personal feelings in the way.

Example: I sat with a founder years ago who was diagnosed with cancer. They were undergoing chemotherapy and experiencing immense personal and professional stress. A proactive way of describing their situation is: "I am experiencing physical exhaustion from chemo and long hours," rather than, "I am broken and a failure." The former reduces fear and interpretation, so we can respond with solutions.

What Is a Small Step I Can Take?

Founders are guilty of going from 0–100, wanting their desired results all at once. With an all-or-nothing mentality, self-care becomes difficult and many founders give up before they start. It becomes another thing to fail at, rather than being gentle with yourself and taking a small step: just 0–1.

Example: The first four months after Keane's passing, my mind and my body were exhausted. I was facing crisis after crisis (e.g. recovering from a car accident, dealing with my mum's cancer) and 0–100 would have been overwhelming. During my grief, I sought a small victory each day, so that I could build momentum toward my goals. In my first month, a win was getting eight hours of sleep. In my third month, a win was attending one in-person event a week.

What Structure Can I Create?

In the startup world, we have structures in place so that every department can operate without us. We have Standard Operating Procedures (SOPs) that allow us to document the processes and metrics to maintain optimal behaviors in the long run. Where is that same rigor and commitment when it comes to our self-care? When we are in crisis, structures matter. Structures are the safety net beneath us, catching us when we fall.

Example: As a mental health leader, I am exposed to stressful and highly charged situations. Thus, structure is vital to my physical and mental well-being. I maintain a daily morning routine called Morning Pages (based on Julia Cameron's book *The Artist's Way*), where I start my day writing three pages by hand. I write down whatever comes to mind, allowing me to release, process, or integrate any lingering emotions from the day before. All meetings and commitments are set in my Google Calendar as well, where I have blocked off three to four sessions at the gym each week for my physical health.

INTERNAL EXERCISE: WHEEL OF LIFE

To create stability, we start by taking stock of our life. How can we know what to improve on if we haven't asked how we're *really* doing? Like a traveler, we must know where we are to get to where we want to go.

My favorite tool for clients is the Wheel of Life. A coaching tool created in the 1960s by Paul J. Meyer, a pioneer in the self-improvement industry, the Wheel of Life assesses you on eight areas of life: Health, Career, Love, Spirituality, Family, Money, Fun, and Friends.[8] Personal *and* professional areas are measured because founders tend to self-sabotage by succeeding at one area of life (usually Career or Money), at the expense of everything else. Operating from all-or-nothing is unhealthy and unsustainable, leaving a founder at risk for a physical or mental breakdown.

Founders aren't robots or machines; we are humans whose minds and bodies require maintenance to stay optimal. Leadership is sustainable only when it is holistic: healthy in multiple or all areas of life.

Instructions:

1. **Category:** Take out a piece of paper. Write down the eight categories (Health, Career, Love, Spirituality, Family, Money, Fun, and Friends) vertically.
2. **Rating:** Rate each category out of 10. How are you actually doing in that area of life? Follow your instincts and write down the first number that comes to mind. As leaders, we may lie or pretend that a category is doing better than it really is. Reasoning and justification are to be avoided. There are no good or bad scores, just high and low scores. We need to be honest with ourselves, so we know where to start.
3. **Stars:** Assess what is working. What people, events, or things stand out to you as personal or professional victories? Where are you doing well?

4. **Stairs:** Assess what is not working. What are you frustrated or complaining about? Where could you improve? Approach Stairs from curiosity rather than making yourself wrong. By removing judgment, it becomes easier to be real with ourselves.

Category	Rating (__/10)	Stars: What did I do well? What should I continue doing?	Stairs: What can I improve on? What should I stop or change?
Health	8	CrossFit three times per week Daily walk for 30 minutes	Eat more veggies Reduce chips
Career	4	Released my podcast Hired team to support me	Should I discontinue or pause the business until COVID-19 is over?
Love	8	Went on five dates this month Put myself out there again	Vulnerability is hard! Work on trusting others and enjoying myself, rather than being so serious
Spirituality	8	Reflect with journaling every morning End my night with prayer	Remember that spirituality is not about doing, but being
Family	8	Call my parents twice a week Started a family WhatsApp group	Reach out more to dad Be more patient when my sister is catching up with me
Money	2	Pivoted my business to an online group model Reach out to five leads on LinkedIn a day	Unable to see clients in-person anymore because of COVID-19 Create a new budget based on my resources and needs
Fun	8	Book one weekend day (Saturday or Sunday) each week for me time Create a list of spots that I want to explore in the city	Say no to additional work commitments, so I have time for fun Be adventurous and try new activities I haven't done before
Friends	6	Book coffee dates with a different friend each week Return to my personal Facebook	Be more consistent in spending time with friends, rather than rescheduling Choose which friendships to grow and which ones to let go of

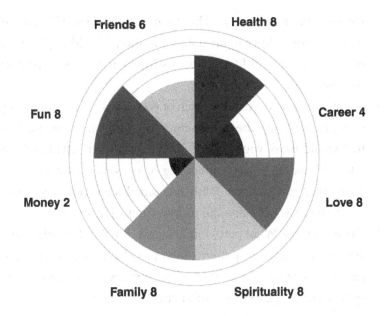

Friends 6   Health 8

Fun 8   Career 4

Money 2   Love 8

Family 8   Spirituality 8

EXTERNAL EXERCISE: NEEDS AND NOURISHMENTS

Breakdowns happen in leadership when we see problems but ignore or deny them. **Avoidance**, a common reason for leadership failure, makes us a victim of circumstance rather than the creator of our lives. In the world of stability, business leaders are willing and able to respond to problems because they have a minimum standard of self-care.

Like a leaky boat, we must patch the holes of our own ship before we focus on others.

Instructions:

1. **Category:** Look at your Wheel of Life. Focus on the category with the lowest score. If you have two or more areas tied, select the one that feels "hardest" to you.

2. **Needs:** Similar to Maslow's Hierarchy of Needs, a **need** is a requirement for your physical, mental, or emotional health. What do you need in this area of life that is missing or insufficient? Be honest with yourself!

3. **Nourishments:** Go through each of your needs, one by one. As you sit with them, use the Nourishments column to write *one* action that would move you forward. Remember that 0–100 is a form of self-sabotage by overcomplicating your solutions and creating unrealistic expectations. With one small step each day, you can break the cycle of Chaos and restore Control in your life.

4. **Observations:** What have you been avoiding? What behaviors do you repeat? Note any patterns in your behavior and thinking that get you stuck in Chaos. With awareness, we can interrupt these patterns and replace them with better behaviors.

Category: Money (2/10)

Needs	Nourishments	Observations
Used up 80% of my life savings during COVID-19.	Spend one hour tomorrow asking my network for job opportunities.	I find outbound sales (creating leads) to be exhausting as an introvert.
Unable to start a family (our first child) and feel like I'm disappointing my partner.	Have a conversation with my partner about my fears around money.	I tend to do things alone; I bottle up my feelings and get upset often.
Currently $3500 in credit card debt.	Call my dad tomorrow and ask for a $2500 loan, which I will pay back in two months.	My parents ask if I'm okay and if they can help, but I lie to them.

PREPARING TO SPRINT

In the competitive field of swimming, there is a turning point in a race where momentum can be gained. It happens at the ends of each pool, where there are walls to push off from. This movement is called the **push-off** or **flip turn**, and it is so critical to performance that swimmers and coaches will train for this single move. Pushing off the wall creates the second highest gain in speed, only next to the very start of the race, where the swimmer pushes off the diving block.[9]

Similar to this wall, this chapter on stability creates the foundation for momentum in our lives. In having a metaphorical ground to stand on, we can move away from fear and victimization, reclaiming some control in our lives. In the next chapter, we build on this foundation by taking responsibility and creating power for ourselves as leaders.

CHAPTER FOUR

INTEGRITY

It was April 2018 and I felt lonely. It was a terrible feeling.

When I was a young girl, Keane and I watched a ton of sci-fi. All the classics like *The Twilight Zone*, *The X-Files*, *Star Trek: The Next Generation*, and *Stargate SG-1*. My dad was a verifiable nerd before nerds were cool. He ran his self-made business and he loved engineering and science.

Even though I had an unusually harsh and adverse childhood, I became successful as an adult. I was popular. I was loved. I used my book smarts to connect with others and make close friends. Lots of friends. I was eclectic and a proficient storyteller, part of multiple friend circles that represented different interests.

Imagine my shock when I went from attending multiple events a week – seeing lots of friends – to nothing. Zip. Nada. My network felt like crickets. No one was calling. No one was texting. I couldn't remember the last time I was invited to a party.

Had I done something wrong?

The thing about grief is that it feels like you are losing your mind. I was reading books on grief, most notably *On Grief and Grieving* by Elisabeth

Kubler-Ross (the foremost expert in the space) and it wasn't enough. I had this giant hole in my chest. I went from being a sibling-entrepreneur of 10 years, with Keane by my side, to nothing. It was inconceivable to imagine a world without the sibling I grew up with.

The more I thought about my potential future, the more depressed I got. It was hard to stomach a future without Keane in it.

My saving grace, the one moment that changed my life, was a friend named Laurel (pseudonym). She was the *one* friend who reached out and she went out of her way. She would ask me how I was really doing. No fluff. In a small way, it felt like the conversations I once had with Keane. Real talk, leaning into my emotions, and making space for the elephant in the room.

I was so thankful to Laurel because she held a safe space for me. This single individual changed the trajectory of my grief. She and I were friends for several years, but it was only after Keane's passing when I realized she had experienced grief too.

Many years ago, Laurel had lost her brother very suddenly and without the chance to say goodbye. Similar to myself, our brothers had passed away during key moments of our lives and they were of similar age (in their twenties) – leaving behind their older sisters. Similar to myself, she had felt alone in her circle of friends as well.

It was Laurel who helped me understand that real talk was a gift and that it was normal for our friends (and sometimes, family) to go quiet during grief. They cared. They just didn't know what to say.

A FRAGILE SOCIETY

In my experiences of mental health, trauma, and grief, what has caused me the most pain has been the loneliness and shame. Not the actual event, but going through the aftermath alone. Of processing its ramifications, stumbling in the darkness.

It felt that way for me the first months after Keane's death. It was terrifying to sit with a future where I would grow old without Keane. It was terrifying to sit with a future where I was the last descendant of our lineage.

I share this experience because this loneliness is killing leaders, either physically or mentally. This experience brings me back to the earliest days of #REALTALK, when 35 founders said they avoided, omitted, or lied in their conversations with co-founders, investors, and even spouses. These people chose to look good (or "save face," as we say in Chinese culture) rather than be real.

By choosing to pretend, they suffered. With their mental and emotional walls still in place, it was hard for others to help.

When I first started this mental health movement, I named it For Founders by Founders. It signified our stand, where we wanted to see tech founders support their own. We wanted to see a world where instead of pretend, leaders of leaders could be supported by each other, their teams, and other stakeholders important to their lives, like their families, their investors, and even their partners.

I knew I stumbled onto something special with this phrase, this message, because word of our work quickly spread. Organically, founders and investors would recommend me to their friends who needed a safe space to share.

They wanted to talk about mental health, just not publicly.

It was only after our first year when I realized the movement needed to be named #REALTALK. What was missing in conversations small and big in the workplace was being **real**. Saying what you mean, being who you are, and following through on commitments. This sentence is the definition of **integrity**, a coaching term for our words and our actions in alignment.

Too often, we hide, pretend, or lie in plain sight. In a world without integrity, we can no longer trust ourselves and others. It creates a world of constant self-doubt and anxiety, leading to our current era of fake news, cancel culture, and rising depression due to social media and influencer culture. Despite being the most connected we have ever been technologically, we are the most disconnected physically, mentally, and emotionally.

Not only that, there are great ramifications for how breaking your integrity, time and time again, affects your mental and emotional state. How it affects the internal dialog in your head and how you see and trust yourself on a daily basis. Speaking from my professional experiences, I had spent many years in the tech industry telling myself that I was an advocate of mental health and yet choosing a lifestyle that didn't honor that at all. I was working 80–100 hours a week and sacrificing family, friends, and relationships in order to make it. Thinking back, it was obvious that living this at-all-costs lifestyle was in complete contradiction to what I said was important in my own life.

As these patterns built up, a pattern of saying one thing and doing another, my trust in myself began to erode. After all, how can you feel confident in yourself and your leadership if you are breaking commitments to yourself day in and day out?

The damage created from being out of integrity is insidious. It is consuming poison, a little bit each day until you break down.

Once you start, it can go downhill quickly. Breaking your promise to go back to the gym, breaking your promise to complete projects on time, breaking your promise to others on responsibilities. Integrity is a powerful double-edged sword that either supercharges our self-leadership by seeing ourselves as the person that honors our word, or tanks our self-leadership by seeing ourselves as the person that is disempowered, making false promises and always falling short.

This breakdown in integrity is also the source of imposter syndrome in our workplaces and in broader society. Common in founder and executive circles, it invokes the question: How could someone be successful on paper, yet feel like a failure inside? A psychological phenomenon, **imposter syndrome** is the chronic condition of self-doubt and fear that one will be caught. The belief that someone will see them for the "fraud" they are.

When we pay attention to our lives as leaders, we begin to see the fragility. Rather than leaning into realness and building the muscle for real talk, we (as a collective) have been going in the opposite direction for decades. We have become reactive, unable to handle large (or even small) stresses in a public arena. This level of fragility also comes with additional consequences, such as an inability to be with dissenting opinions and intense emotions without being triggered or feeling attacked. Leaders in these situations end up behaving in ways that are non-conducive, such as reacting, attacking, and lashing out, rather than the level of steadiness that can build bridges.

The fact is, workplaces (along with their leaders) have lacked resilience. We have become a fragile society, disempowered in helping ourselves and others. We have become a shadow of our former selves.

THE TRAGEDY
OF TONY HSIEH

As the leader of #REALTALK, I am privy to the deaths in the tech industry. Over the years, founders and investors will disclose colleagues who have completed suicide or suddenly passed, having struggled with conditions like depression, bipolar disorder, or addiction beforehand.

In recent years, one individual who has stood out is Tony Hsieh. He was the CEO of Zappos, an online shoe and clothing company. A startup unicorn, Zappos was sold to Amazon for $1.2 billion in 2009. Hsieh was the CEO of Zappos since 2001, and he revolutionized the tech industry by focusing on company culture, which was unheard of at the time. Listed on *Fortune*'s 100 Best Companies to Work For, tech founders would regularly tour the Zappos headquarters to learn how to create a customer-first culture.

His approach was so influential that Hsieh wrote a book called *Delivering Happiness: A Path to Profits, Passion and Purpose*, which ended up number one on the *New York Times* bestsellers list. He regularly spoke of spreading joy to employees and customers and doing good in business. In the world of tech, he was seen as a benevolent and generous leader.

What many people didn't know was that Hsieh was struggling behind the scenes. In November 2020, the world was shocked when outlets reported Tony Hsieh's sudden passing. He was 46 and the circumstances of his death were unsettling. He passed away from smoke inhalation, locked in a storage shed attached to the house. Media reports shared that Hsieh struggled with depression and substance use months prior to this death.[1] Grammy-nominated singer Jewel sent Hsieh a letter, concerned about his mental health and the people enabling his lifestyle of heavy partying and drug use.

Further details emerged in January 2021 when *Forbes* reported, "It was likely Hsieh was intoxicated when the fire started, as he was surrounded by smoldering cigarettes, a marijuana pipe, a bottle of Fernet and several canisters of Whip-It nitrous oxide, which Hsieh was known to have used in his final months."[2]

I share the details of Hsieh's story because his death could have been prevented. As a business leader, Hsieh made an incredible impact on the future of work by bringing a level of positivity and care to workplaces around the world. His success became an example for other leaders to do the same.

However, the fact is that in most workplaces today, real talk continues to be scarce. Rather than calling people forward and naming a problem for what it is, we bystand and enable. **Bystanding** is the practice of turning a blind eye, unwilling to help someone in need. **Enabling** is the practice of encouraging dysfunctional behavior, such as allowing an alcoholic to continue their lifestyle.

We allow colleagues and friends to struggle alone, pretending not to see or care. This trend is especially concerning because we are experiencing a time of unprecedented change and stress. Imagine the conversations that are happening at a global level on artificial intelligence. In 2023, Goldman Sachs published a global economic report stating that 300 million jobs this decade will be displaced by AI.[3] Pursuing innovation, following through our commitments, and doing hard things is no longer a nice-to-have: it is essential. Innovation is no longer optional for any organization, where many decades ago, people treated it as a bonus activity if there were additional funds that year.

All leaders (and their companies) must meet or surpass the pace of innovation in order to survive. I believe leaders are underestimating the challenges we face this decade, perhaps even this century. All businesses will require leaders of leaders that are no longer "just putting in the hours," but have the bravery, ingenuity, and stamina to last in a world that feels ruthless in every arena: from the professional to the personal.

This apathy, bystanding, and enabling needs to stop, before we lose more leaders to such tragedies.

Despite Hsieh's contributions to the world and the financial resources he had (his $700 million net worth), he battled his mental illness alone. Even though he was surrounded by so many people physically, I would argue that he was mentally and emotionally alone and that many of the people in his life didn't have his back and acted out of integrity.

While Hsieh's life ended in tragedy, this situation is more common than we think: hiding, lying, and pretending with the people we know and the people who care about us.

Where do we go from here as leaders of leaders?

THE IMPORTANCE OF LISTENING

When my brother passed in 2017, I decided to get my coaching certification. I had three certifications in Special Education and two degrees based in social and developmental psychology, but I wanted more tools in the toolbox. To take on mental health in the tech industry, I needed to prepare.

I researched for several months and ended up training under Michael Neill. He is known as the "coach's coach" and his clientele includes global celebrities, CEOs, and royalty. With 30 years of experience, Neill is internationally renowned and has shaped the Executive Coaching space. His school specializes in Transformative Coaching.

I remember my first week of training with Neill. One of our first assignments was listening in pairs: one person would speak and the other person would listen. Neill's definition was particular: listening didn't mean "not speaking," but letting go of the thoughts, assumptions, and intentions in our head.

There was no goal. There was no fixing. There was no solving. All we had to do was listen. That moment transformed my life.

I was in a brightly lit room, surrounded by 50 or so people, and sitting in front of me was a man who started sharing. As the minutes went on, for the first time in years, the noise in my head disappeared. It was like there was cotton in my ears and now I was hearing surround sound. I realized that in conversations with people, new or old, my mental chatter was saying, *What's wrong? What do they want? What do I need to fix?* I was problem-solving and risk-mitigating before they said their first word. I became aware that my "listening" style was influenced by my childhood, where I was solving multiple crises and caretaking for my family much of the time.

More importantly, in doing this exercise again and again, I realized how loud my inner dialog was. The dialog that was asking questions, that was brainstorming solutions, that was imagining and mapping scenarios in my head. There was even a dialog that wasn't asking or solving at all, just doing commentary (like a sports game) and reacting. It was both illuminating and horrifying to realize that I was like that in every conversation: with friends, with family, and even with strangers.

Listening, but not really hearing. I was not listening at all.

How do you listen in your life? As leaders of leaders, we spend a lot of time in our heads, repeating past stories and talking to ourselves. We know what our co-founders, investors, or spouses are going to say . . . or do we? The irony is that many people become leaders like yourself because you've been able to anticipate people's problems and even their needs.

In embodying listening, we need to unlearn the habits that got us here, but won't get us to the next level.

This invitation is the simple truth behind the #REALTALK movement: we are not real with ourselves and others. And in order to be real with others, we need to restore our ability to listen and actually hear. Without this condition being met, how can we ever hope to act with integrity – for our words to be met and lived by our actions? If we could be real by sharing and listening to one another, we could transform the workplace mental health crisis as we know it.

THE BUSINESS VALUE OF LISTENING

There are readers experiencing this chapter and resisting the work. I was once like you. Listening requires intention and care, but it's worth it.

Listening can be the greatest business asset there is.

#REALTALK has high-profile founders and investors who have pledged their mental health stories about depression, grief, addiction, and more. When we released those stories, the tech industry was shocked. I was receiving emails on a daily basis from business leaders, saying that they "didn't know." They were reading stories of friends and colleagues they had known for years, but they were learning for the first time about their struggles with mental health.

We think we know people. We don't.

Since the first day of #REALTALK, our work has been more than just another mental health campaign. Our work is risk mitigation.

Real talk is the most powerful risk mitigation tool there is. Listening and identifying a moment, situation, or problem with clarity and speed creates business opportunities too. This listening allowed Keane and I to share a decade-long relationship as sibling entrepreneurs. We went into spaces, entire communities where listening had disappeared, and we opened our hearts. We allowed the people in those communities to teach us, to show us what was important to them and the businesses we could build.

This business potential is what underlies Diversity, Equity, and Inclusion (DEI) in the tech industry. People sometimes see DEI as feelings, morality, or pandering, coming from right or wrong.

DEI's potential goes way beyond this. In having people of diverse backgrounds, such as a Black male founder or a single mom founder, listening creates new thinking. Instead of perpetuating the same frameworks of success and money, they re-evaluate their assumptions and co-create solutions as a community.

Listening does not just benefit underrepresented leaders, but everyone. In my day-to-day work, most of my colleagues or peers are White men. Listening has been an incredible tool to connect with leaders that look like me and who also don't, so that we are creating shared spaces where we can work toward one mission. I feel so strongly about surrounding yourself with and listening to different perspectives that I practice this in my own life. When I mentor women leaders, I tell them that it is important to have different types of circles. Not just circles of women, but also being in spaces where men reside, or even people of differing roles or backgrounds.

As a society, we have spent too long siloing ourselves in echo chambers and not wanting to listen. The reality is that this way of operating is unsustainable, especially for leaders who aspire for greatness. Building and especially scaling a company will require people of different skillsets, upbringings, and even networks. If you are the kind of leader who only feels empowered or confident when you are surrounded by people that look like you, you've already lost the war.

The fact is: there is a power to listening for the sake of listening. To listen from empty.

Listening creates a **paradigm shift**, where the normal way of thinking or doing is challenged by a new and different way. A paradigm shift is relevant to **transformation**, which alters the nature and core of something, versus **change**, which is small and incremental progress.

Real talk is in the business of *transformation*. It is transformation that creates innovation and allows leaders of leaders and their companies to flourish, just like Buckminster Fuller advocated so long ago.

By operating from a place of integrity, in really hearing people's truths and seeing the situation for what it is, we begin to have the information necessary for transformation. We begin to see things from a place of first principles, right at the root, so that we can address problems and issues at hand.

FROM LISTENING TO SPEAKING

At #REALTALK, we focus on communication as the key skill because it has transformative and exponential impact. If we look at our daily lives, both personal and professional, most if not all opportunities start with a conversation and the ability to listen. This leadership ability is necessary in a world where we need solutions that can work for massive amounts of people with limited time and resources.

With a foundation of Listening, we can talk about Speaking. As humans, when we get close to something tender or vulnerable, we begin to hide. Wearing the mask is a form of self-protection, especially after trauma or mistrust. Every leader of leaders has been through a scenario where they placed their trust in something or someone, only for that trust to be broken.

However, for us to effectively show up as leaders, we cannot stay there. We cannot stay in the space of mistrust.

To break the cycle of suffering, we need to shift from shame to real talk. Rather than carrying a story about being broken, being wrong, and being "not good enough," we share to transform ourselves.

We show ourselves that we are whole and complete, despite our previous mistakes. We embrace being human.

In working with many founders, their mental and emotional suffering has persisted not because of a lack of resources but an unwillingness to share themselves. This unwillingness to share is the root of our problems around integrity and self-leadership. After all, if you are pretending to be okay, how do people see you? How do people support you when they don't know you're struggling?

They don't. They leave you alone to deal with it yourself.

A few years ago, I sat in a room of CEOs from multiple industries, where one individual (who ran a highly successful, multi-million-dollar business) talked at length about the pressure they felt. The loneliness. Despite being the market leader in their industry, they felt like they didn't fit anywhere. They were constantly worried about whether they would be supported as a leader, and the worst part was, it affected what they thought of themselves because they were so out of integrity, and they knew it.

When we speak from a place of realness, we can begin to depend on ourselves and others again. We can restore our integrity by having our words match our actions, starting with ourselves. There are three levels of Speaking from lowest to highest impact:

1. **Thinking (Internal):** Our thoughts are a running dialog, a 24/7 stream of words about every topic imaginable: our jobs, being hungry, or disliking the shirt we are wearing today. For instance, Dr. Fred Luskin of Stanford University discovered that a human being has approximately 60 000 thoughts per day, 90% of which are repetitive.[4] We are constantly speaking to ourselves, carrying the

same patterns, beliefs, or thoughts from the previous day. Not only that, this mental chatter is occurring even when you aren't saying anything aloud, like my example with Michael Neill earlier in this chapter.

2. **Writing (External):** What people read about us, from media articles to social media, is often their first impression of us. In psychology, the strongest and most lasting impressions are the first impression and the last impression. It is often why as a keynote speaker I am hired to either open the conference or close the conference. I share this because as a speaker, I am asked for my biography and stage intro, and these materials are what shape the initial listening of my audience. Research based on the Harvard Study of Communications, conducted by social psychologist Dr. Amy Cuddy, found that it only takes seven seconds to make a first impression on another person.[5]

3. **Speaking (External):** When we are physically face-to-face with others, speaking aloud or signing is our primary form of communication. It includes verbal and nonverbal cues, with only 7% of our communication based on the actual words spoken. In an iconic study by Dr. Albert Mehrabian, he found there was a 55-38-7 rule with communication: 55% from body language, 38% from the tone of voice, and 7% from actual words spoken.[6] Even though it may be hard to accept, people can sense when we are saying something we don't mean or something that isn't true. There's a heaviness, an awkwardness, or a something-doesn't-quite-click impression that can create distance instead of connection with another person.

As we shift from theory to application, the following exercises will strengthen your muscles for listening and speaking, so that you can bring more integrity to your words and actions. I invite you to take these exercises on fully, so that you can create a healthy and adaptive foundation for self-leadership.

INTERNAL EXERCISE: LISTENING FROM EMPTY

To create the space for Listening, we need to evaluate our relationship to it.

As founders, we can be stubborn and prideful by assuming that we are effective and willing listeners. How well are we listening to others, much less ourselves? How can we improve the way we communicate and connect with one another?

Instructions:

1. Find a podcast episode (20 minutes minimum) of a leader whom you've resisted. For example, if you are Left-leaning, you could search for an episode from a popular Right-leaning commentator.
2. **What I Heard:** Listen to the podcast. As the host or guest is speaking, pay attention to your listening: the dialog that is going on in your head. What is your little voice saying? Write down your understanding of the podcast. Make sure to write down the time stamp, so that you can refer back to it.
3. **What They Actually Said:** Afterward, return to those time stamps. Re-listen to one or two minutes of each segment and write down an impartial quotation, with as little interpretation or opinion from you as possible. Impartial information includes numbers and statistics, rather than your opinions or stories.
4. Compare the results from the two columns. Are you really listening? What is coming up for you as you are looking at this table?

Time stamp	What I heard	What they actually said
11:25	"He thinks the Left are stupid. He dislikes anything related to social assistance."	"Actually, UBI [universal basic income] is an interesting concept, but how would you implement that? Many Americans are on disability and stay on disability for the rest of their lives."

EXTERNAL EXERCISE: SPOKEN VS. UNSPOKEN

Building on the last exercise, this one is focused on External communication: looking at how you interact with other people. What are you saying (Spoken) or not saying (Unspoken) each day? Is there alignment between what is real for you and what you are saying? Or does most of your conversation remain in the hidden and pretend?

Instructions:

1. Select a date when you will conduct this full-day exercise. Set a timer on your phone or watch, so that it beeps every 30 minutes.

2. **Spoken:** At each 30-minute mark, write down the words you wrote or spoke in that conversation. What were you saying to other people?

3. **Unspoken:** Only after filling out the Spoken column, write down any thoughts or feelings you hid away. Is there something else you wanted to say? If you said everything you wanted to say, in the way you meant to say it, leave this column blank.

4. **Observation:** Allow at least an hour before you go to bed. Take this time to reflect on your conversations today. Write down your Observations.

5. Score your Totals for the Spoken and Unspoken columns. All rows with a filled Unspoken column count as one point for Unspoken conversation. It means there is a dissonance or gap between what was real for you *and* what you shared with others. All other rows count as one point for Spoken conversation.

6. Look at the ratio between Spoken to Unspoken. How often are you communicating with integrity? How often do you hide, omit, or pretend in communication? Does it surprise you? What are you noticing for yourself?

Time of day	Spoken: What do people see from you? What are you showing and sharing with others?	Unspoken: What is real that continues to remain unexpressed? What is the elephant in the room?	Observation: What do you notice? Is there a gap between the spoken and the unspoken?
10:00 a.m.	"I am successful. I am a keynote speaker represented by a bureau."	"I feel like a failure. I haven't booked a gig since the pandemic started."	I don't know if or when I will feel ready to share. I feel a lot of pressure to make my business work.
10:30 a.m.	"I can handle this. I am capable and I have structures in place."		
11:00 a.m.	"I love my partner. I am so lucky to have them."	"I wish our relationship was more exciting. Why do I keep pulling away?"	I share truthfully with my best friend but with no one else, not even my partner.
Total	1	2	

LETTING GO OF BEING RIGHT

So much about being a leader has to do with our pregame: the preparations we make before we enter a space or a conversation. Similar to athletes, we must be intentional about our words and our actions. In a world where people are scared and reactive, we must hold ourselves to a higher standard.

Our world is hurting and as leaders of leaders in the workplace, we have a chance to show up and lead.

To lead in this way, integrity is of utmost importance. We started with #REALTALK with Me, a conversation with the self, because people are tired of pretend. People are disappointed – of leaders making promises and not following through. We need better, and it starts with holding higher standards for our words and our actions.

As we restore our realness in the way we listen and speak, we invite you to be *real* instead of right. Great leadership comes from honesty and humility, not ego.

CHAPTER FIVE

WORKABILITY

I t was July 2018, and I was dreading the summer. I was based in Toronto, Canada, with long winters brought by heavy snow and cold winds. For a city that spent much of its year in winter, summer was a big deal.

Summer was associated with happiness, with lightness, with new memories built with family and friends. It was a time of parties, sunsets, and cottaging.

This July felt different. It was my first summer without my brother.

I wasn't sure what to do with this.

Summers were our favorite times as siblings. It was vacation season, so our workload would lighten. It meant an opportunity for us to try new restaurants and visit our favorite spots. Keane and I had an obsession with The Keg and Red Lobster (a childhood tradition), where we would shake off our entrepreneurial baggage and lighten up. We would be two siblings, chatting about life, dating, and the normal things outside of work.

I was grateful that the chaos had lightened, but there was still an intensity to my day-to-day life. It was the aftermath of my brother's death and my mum's cancer.

My mother had survived two surgeries and she had started chemo and radiation. It meant daily visits to the hospital and coordinating with doctors, nurses, and other staff. I was building out my mental health movement, formerly called For Founders by Founders, at the time. I was having intense conversations with tech founders, investors, and executive directors.

Having those conversations was like opening a can of worms; now that tech leaders started talking about mental health, I had to follow through.

On top of that, our household was stressful. I was living with my parents as we recovered physically, mentally, and emotionally as a family. My mother's surgeries were serious, so she couldn't walk or put pressure on her stomach. It required several months of full-time recovery. My dad and I moved a spare bed to the first floor so that the kitchen and the front door were accessible.

She couldn't walk up the stairs without pain.

As much as I wanted to help my parents, living in that house was tough. Triggering.

The family house held painful memories for me. I had spent years of my childhood in an unstable and combative environment, where shouting was commonplace and understanding was hard to come by. Everyone in our family was struggling and grieving after Keane's death, but I was particularly worried for my dad. Our family came from a culture where conversations on mental health were considered taboo, especially for men.

It felt like my childhood all over again. Everything felt too much, all the time, and all I wanted was myself and my family to find safe harbor.

A GAME OF RISK

When we are overwhelmed or fall into fear, life can feel unbearable. Unsolvable.

At the end of a tumultuous 2020, I recorded a tender episode for the #REALTALK podcast with a dear friend and champion of ours, Edwin Frondozo, co-founder and CEO of Slingshot VoIP. Edwin and I have known each other for many years because we are both tech founders who are also podcasters, wanting to make the world a better place through our platforms. In that interview, he and I talked about the importance of a **flashpoint**: a moment of great conflict and great opportunity. The word flashpoint encapsulated 2020 perfectly.

In fact, #REALTALK started from a flashpoint: Keane's death.

In navigating several, often traumatic flashpoints over two decades, I have learned a thing or two about bouncing back. I have observed that individuals, especially leaders of leaders, are resistant to change – much less transformation. Like many other things, humans tend to default to the status quo, where it requires time, effort, and sometimes even money to reassess and make the decisions your life needs. As a result, many wait until a breakdown or crisis in their business or in their life before they look in the mirror. A game of luck – many leaders operate on the "I hope that doesn't happen to me" attitude to stay afloat.

That is a dangerous game. When will your luck run out? What will you do when you reach a level of responsibility and success, where consistent, high-performing action is necessary to survive, much less thrive?

In the venture capital world, investors are hedging their bets all the time. Bets on the future, on which companies will be the next unicorns to 10 times their investment. Venture capitalists (VCs) are in the game of innovation and have been for many decades, where they win by investing in companies long before they become mainstream. This mentality of going first (and having to make critical decisions with high conviction) is an important muscle that all VCs, especially the best ones, do.

According to research by Startup Genome, a world-leading innovation firm, 90% of all startups fail.[1] Innovation is incredibly difficult to do as a first-mover and to do it with scale. In the report *Business Employment Dynamics*, the US Bureau of Labor found that startups exhibit:

- Twenty percent failure rate by the end of year one
- Thirty percent failure rate by the end of year two
- Fifty percent failure rate by the end of year five
- Seventy percent failure rate by the end of year ten

In the world of business, all organizations are now focused on the future. Every organization feels the pressure of thriving or dying, especially in a fast-paced world where innovation is the name of the game. It is the difference between standing still (doing nothing and being helpless) and **still standing:** being the business and eventually market leader that outlasts and surpasses all the rest. It is the latter that motivates leaders like myself to be in the world of VC, for the chance of investing in and working with world-changing, market-defining companies.

However, in order to compete in this game, you cannot bury your head in the sand, hoping things will tide over. This is especially true for leaders of leaders like yourself, where internal and external stakeholders look to your example for how to act and respond.

Like the scrappy and resilient way that startups operate, we can take back the reins. We can take ownership of our mistakes by asking ourselves what is working and not working. That is the power of **workability:** restoring function in every situation or environment, so we can make our circumstances work for us.

In my work with startups and even corporations, I see how often workplaces have settled for dysfunction. I have seen workplaces that continue to build teams and even cultures that have not worked for anyone (especially the employees) in a long time. Employees fear that if they speak out and share what is not working, that they will be vilified. Judged. Punished. There is even apathy that can occur, telling themselves not to care in order to reduce the feeling of harm that comes their way.

Instead of going full-in and rising to the occasion as a leader, they shrink. They self-sabotage and take themselves out of the game, before someone else can. It is self-destructive and creates low-performing or emotionally fragile teams as a result.

A huge part of our mission at #REALTALK is risk mitigation. Workability is risk mitigation, where there is a willingness to see breakdowns in your performance and to take action in the now. By being real, we can see problems (and opportunities) early on, so we have the ability and time to respond.

What is working or not working in your life?

HOW WE SELF-SABOTAGE

Most people settle for average or even mediocre lives. We tell ourselves that our relationship, our business, or even our health is working when it is not. In looking back at Tony Hsieh's passing, I wonder how many people around him settled for "okay" and the dysfunction in his life.

To stop this cycle of dysfunction, we need to understand our **loops.** A term from my friend Jason Brown, general partner at Misfits Collective, humans are engaged in deep-seated patterns in how they see, think, and operate in the world. When we are feeling down, we are susceptible to upset, drama, and even victimization, all forms of self-sabotage.

Over the decades, one of my favorite self-development books is *The Big Leap* by Dr. Gay Hendricks. Hendricks is a Stanford psychologist and a renowned coach. In his work with high-performing leaders, he noticed a pattern: people self-sabotaged the closer they got to success.

He called this phenomenon the **Upper Limit Problem**, saying, "Each of us has an inner thermostat setting that determines how much love, success, and creativity we allow ourselves to enjoy. When we exceed our inner thermostat setting, we will often do something to sabotage ourselves, causing us to drop back into the old, familiar zone where we feel secure."[2]

In other words, innate in humans is a resistance toward happiness because when things go well, we worry about what will go wrong. Even physiologically, humans gravitate toward normal, where each function (like body temperature and blood pressure) has a **set point**: a value where the normal range fluctuates.

Beyond a certain deviation, change becomes hard. The new set point we are hoping to keep (like a new career or relationship) feels hard or even unnatural to maintain at first, as if we are forcing things. As we go toward a new dream, a new goal, or a new level of performance, we have a set point.

For leaders of leaders, the Upper Limit Problem is our mental, emotional, and financial set point. We settle for "good enough" or "okay," rather than a successful *and* healthy life. We give up right before the finish line and we often under-prepare in terms of the resources we need to see things through. This pattern of self-sabotage has shown up in most of my clients.

In understanding our nature as human beings, we realize why we have resisted change. We realize why we have resisted the conversation on mental health.

Dr. James Prochaska and Dr. Carlo DiClemente are the leading experts in the treatment and prevention of addictive behaviors. Their work is important to me because I serve on the board for the Canadian Mental Health Association (CMHA), where many of our clients struggle with addiction. Prochaska and DiClemente's research studied alcoholic patients focused on behavioral change. Known as the **Transtheoretical Model,** they discovered that a cyclical pattern (like a staircase) represents how people change their unhealthy behavior.[3] There are five Stages of Change in this order:

1. **Pre-Contemplation:** Unwilling or unable to change
2. **Contemplation:** Aware of the problem, with no commitment to action
3. **Preparation:** Intent on taking action in the next 30 days
4. **Action:** Behavior change for less than six months
5. **Maintenance:** Sustained change, with gains consolidated

At the end of the cycle, there is the possibility of **Termination,** full confidence in maintaining change, or **Relapse,** the recurrence of old behavior. In health programs focused on addictive behaviors, such as smoking, alcohol, and weight, relapse is often listed. It recognizes that 100% cessation of the unwanted behavior is unlikely, but with every cycle experienced, the relapse is shorter and less intense.

Through this research, the practice of workability and "real talk" is not a one-done deal. It requires intentional communication and action, along with responsibility. It requires self-leadership, where we have the courage to admit when a situation or relationship is no longer working for us. Real talk is a muscle that strengthens with every practice and every fall, so that we can let go of what no longer serves us.

By asking ourselves, *What is working and not working?*, we move away from the right/wrong language that causes loops of self-sabotage. We move away from blame or judgment to a willingness to see the situation for what it is. We create a shared language for creating solutions.

Knowing the power of workability, let's learn how to use it.

THE WORLD OF WORKABILITY

To make workability simple, it asks a single question, "What is working or not working in _____?" It could be in business, in relationships, in health, or more. When something is working, you are achieving the results you set out to achieve. When something is not working, that area of life is plagued by emotions like disappointment, frustration, or resentment.

This conversation links to our Wheel of Life exercise in Chapter Three, where we rated the quality of our life in eight areas, scoring each of them out of 10.

To restore workability to your life, there are three coaching distinctions. Remember, a **distinction** is a simple and immediate way to clarify your thinking, by labeling what something is and is not.

At #REALTALK, my team is trained in distinctions. We have professional facilitators who are trained in mental health and/or diversity, equity, and inclusion. These skills have been essential to navigating emotions and even trauma in a space, in order to mitigate risks for the individual and the group. When I speak of risks, individuals may feel that sharing inside their workplace isn't safe, so we create a container for positive and solution-focused discussion. We use these skills in our team, in our community, and especially with clients.

As leaders of leaders, the distinctions of workability create a powerful way to lead. Looking back at the #REALTALK Leadership model, workability is the last stage of #REALTALK with Me, shifting you from Chaos (Survive) to Control (Cope). Instead of putting out fires, leadership becomes responding at the moment.

The word **responding** is an intentional choice because it means having the time or space to truly assess a situation, before making an informed or best choice on how to respond. This behavior is in contrast to **reacting**, where we are defaulting to hardwired behaviors or patterns (such as lashing out, overworking, or panicking), leaving our people less empowered than when they started.

With this intentional use of language, we reduce misunderstandings. Think of communication like water: waves flowing in and out. As we interact with ourselves and others, we have the Sending waves and the Receiving waves. Sending is when we share our message with others, while Receiving is when we listen to others speak.

In every conversation, we navigate what was said (Sending) and what we understood (Receiving). Sometimes, we get these waves confused when we bring our own biases into the conversation.

Distinctions become like fences, allowing us to portion off things, so we can correctly point at pieces of the conversation and say, "Do you see what I'm seeing? What do you think of this?" Here are three distinctions on workability:

Problem vs. Story

Move away from the Story and our interpretation of the events, and talk about the Problem. When we are upset, we stay in the Story by dramatizing what happened and sharing, "It's their fault!" or "They should have known better!" When we are upset, we are listening for drama rather than solutions, since Story focuses on the past and Problem focuses on the present. In schools and the media, examples of healthy communication are rare. We are bombarded by reality TV shows where characters escalate problems by being "right," rather than being real.

By focusing on the Problem, we shift from ourselves to an "external" topic that you can point to. Rather than pointing at each other and creating the opening for blame, all parties are focused on discussing the problem, with the purpose of reaching a shared understanding or resolution. #REALTALK serves this function, acting as a facilitator or middleman between two parties, such as a founder-founder or a founder-investor communication. It creates the opening to take responsibility for any dysfunction in the workplace or in your life.

Responsibility vs. Avoidance

In the early days of #REALTALK, Avoidance was cited by founders as their number one reason for business failure. In psychology, **Avoidance** is a maladaptive behavior of escaping or disconnecting from reality, causing the long-term outcome to remain unchanged. Restoring workability in our lives requires **responsibility.** Responsibility is the timely willingness to discuss a problem and the role we played in its dysfunction. It is an adaptive way to deal with a stressor, embodying traits of Growth mindset and listening from empty.

At #REALTALK, we have a saying, "Being a leader means leading when no one else wants to." In the tech industry, the conversation on

Black Lives Matter has shrunk leaders and expanded others. A similar wave is now happening in the workplace for other topics, like burnout and change resistance, where our people are tired and yet there is still the pressure to innovate. For leaders turning a blind eye, breakdowns are beginning to occur in their teams and their organizations, where stakeholders (like employees and even customers) are calling them forward on their behavior.

Complete vs. Incomplete

Architect and futurist Buckminster Fuller has been the inspiration behind the term workability. He studied the functionality of buildings, looking at their structural integrity. The quality of our lives can be akin to a house. When we look at our "house," is the structure complete or are the beams falling apart? When we leave promises, projects, or problems incomplete, such as partially doing them, it becomes harder to move on. We keep holding on to our past, dragging this baggage into future conversations. The more things that are incomplete, the more baggage to manage in the future.

Incomplete events feed our triggers. For example, seeing an ex-spouse or a former co-founder can be upsetting if there was a messy breakup or if there wasn't a satisfying close. People handle Completion poorly, especially when it involves other people, where they wait until crisis to share the things they needed to say. This pattern is especially true in the workplace, where issues can get shoved under the rug and the tension begins to build. I see this too often in my speaking clients, where I am working with their CEOs to repair the rollout of an innovation strategy already communicated to their direct reports, who don't want do it.

If we truly want to innovate and to thrive while doing it, we need to do better.

THE STANDARDS YOU HOLD

To create workability in your life, especially for extended periods of time, there is another factor that leaders need to consider: our standards. As a senior executive, I am a part of several communities and confidential circles surrounded by other executives, where we support each other on difficult decisions. Should I fire this employee? Should I stop working with this client? Should I consider downsizing my business?

One of the things I have noticed is how standards play into the patterns and responses around crisis. We started this book with #REALTALK with Me because we need to restore stability, integrity, and workability in our lives first, before we can lead our teams and eventually our organizations. When I was working with tech CEOs daily at #REALTALK, I found that so many of these crises (especially when founders couldn't take the stress anymore and wanted to "end" it) had to do with tolerating situations that were below their standards. Tolerating and staying in situations that weren't good or healthy for them because deep down, these leaders didn't believe they deserved more or that better existed.

As a tech CEO, one of the most painful lessons I learned was that leading high-performing organizations isn't about being nice. Growing up as a female, there was a lot of emphasis on being nice, on taking care of others, of sacrificing yourself in order to help the people around you (even if it was a detriment to yourself). This is a socialization pattern that is passed down to our girls and our women on a regular basis.

For many years, I would have teams that were good but not great. Just not enough to get to the next level. I would have team members who I really treasured and wanted them to do well, and I'd spend hours mentoring them and then fixing their mistakes myself. Only when that low standard of performance became unbearable, did I consider letting go of that team member.

It took a long time to hold high standards for myself. To realize that as CEO, I deserve and demand to be supported. That I demand that the people around me show up as leaders, and that I'm not showing up as their therapist or even their mommy. And to heal the guilt around moving on or away from people that no longer served me, who held me back from going to the next level.

Where have your standards fallen? Where have you tolerated situations that are nearly unbearable, only because you are scared of the fallout? Scared of what people will think? Scared if you deserve or will receive better?

It is when things are no longer working that the deep work starts. Where we tell ourselves that we will innovate and we will thrive, yet tolerating behavior, situations, and people that are below our standards. And yes, it matters that we do this with a level of integrity not just in one area of life, but in as many areas as possible.

If we hold high standards in one area of life (think the Wheel of Life), and let go of our standards in other areas, the dissonance will become increasingly obvious to you and eventually others. It shows up as feeling out of integrity or feeling like a hypocrite, disappointed in yourself and others. Maintaining our standards as leaders matters and makes the difference in who and how we show up in the workplace and in our lives.

KNOWING WHEN TO LEAVE

Before we go to our exercises, I want to share one thing. There may be some of you reading this book that are in situations, personal and professional, that have come to a tipping point. A fork in the road where a decision is imminent and the pressure has become unbearable.

When we speak of workability, of making our lives work for us, it is *not* about prolonging a situation. There will be times where restoring workability is about leaving: saying no and releasing that opportunity, that situation, or that person. It is important to highlight because too often, people stay in roles or situations that they should have left a long time ago, leading to the prolonged feeling of "not working for me" we spoke of.

Knowing when to leave (aka quit) is one of the most important skills you can learn as a leader of leaders. Unlike the stories we have in the media, there is actually a great amount of benefit and self-awareness in knowing when to leave a situation, instead of suffering and acting like a martyr. When we build this muscle for ourselves, it allows us to address things immediately and to leave situations gracefully, rather than exiting or lashing out at others in a dramatic fashion.

Another book that is near and dear to me is Seth Godin's *The Dip*. In writing my book, I had the opportunity to chat with him briefly through email, in order to ask for his testimonial (thank you Seth!). In *The Dip*, Godin talks about the fact that winners (high performers) quit the right stuff at the right time.[4] They are serial quitters: they know when to quit, in order to free themselves up to pursue something else. To be great, to be exceptional at something, means being focused and being committed. If you are constantly in situations or responsibilities that are incomplete or no longer serve you, then it's important to quit the wrong things.

Additionally, Godin speaks of the fact that when you are in this **dip** (a moment where things are extremely painful), you need to be real with yourself. You need to assess whether what you are doing is worth the cost right now and the payoff on the other side. If the payoff isn't significant enough (and yes, this relates to our standards and how we hold ourselves as leaders), then we should quit.

Too often we allow and accept circumstances that are tolerable. Being tolerable or even average won't cut it anymore, not in this economic and technological climate. It's not the winning attitude for business or innovation, where there will be big winners and also big losers, depending on the standards you hold and what you will focus on or let go.

Where are you continuing to stay, when you should quit? What situations are you still in that are no longer serving you?

INTERNAL EXERCISE: RADICAL PRIORITIZATION

If we have breakdowns in performance, emotions like resentment, blame, and disappointment are present. We must look critically at the gap between our words and our actions to restore function in that area. Do our actions match the results we want to create? Have our actions created a life of workability?

Our actions reflect our priorities. They reflect what we value.

Instructions:

1. **Activity:** Spend one week tracking how you spend your time. Track each activity.
2. **Time Frame:** When you are switching to a new activity, write the start and end times.
3. **Time Commitment:** Right before bed, calculate the time (in minutes) it took for each activity.
4. Repeat this process each day. If observations come up, write them in the **Notes** section.

Activity	Time frame	Time commitment	Notes
Reading reddit	9:30–10:15 a.m.	45 minutes	
Washing dishes	10:15–10:45 a.m.	30 minutes	
Taking meetings	10:45 a.m.–3:00 p.m.	5 hours, 15 minutes (315 minutes)	Work meetings are usually unproductive, yet most of my 9–5 schedule is meetings

Post-Week Calculations:

1. **Highlight:** Prepare markers or highlighters with a minimum of four different colors.

2. **Categorize:** Pick one color and highlight all activities that match that "category." Don't overthink this. Highlight as quickly as you can. What activities group well together?
3. **Repeat:** Once you have exhausted that category, pick the next color. Repeat step 2 until all activities are accounted for. The result should be the creation of several categories.
4. **Calculate:** For each category, add the Time Commitments together. How long did you spend on each category?
5. **Percentage:** A week is 10 080 minutes. For each category, determine the percentage of time spent on each.

Reflection:

1. **Most:** On which category do you spend the most time?
2. **Least:** On which category do you spend the least time?
3. **Surprise:** Which category surprised you the most? Why?
4. **Expect:** Are the categories what you expected? Are there any categories that are missing?
5. **Rank:** List your categories from most to least time. How do they match up with your priorities?
6. **Prioritize:** Label each category as Continue or Stop, with the intention of creating a more workable life. Realign your schedule by making adjustments to your activities.

EXTERNAL EXERCISE: TAKING RESPONSIBILITY

In Chapter Three, we were introduced to the Wheel of Life, which assesses our quality of life in eight areas: Health, Career, Love, Spirituality, Family, Money, Fun, and Friends. This exercise builds on that foundation.

To restore workability and assess performance, it requires **responsibility**. It means moving ourselves from words into actions and fulfilling the steps required. As leaders, we often declare goals or make promises and fail to follow through. How can we restore our power and our effectiveness as leaders? How can we make sure that our leadership works?

Instructions:

1. **Lowest:** Identify the lowest-scored areas from your Wheel of Life. Write down four of those areas and their scores out of 10.
2. **Not Working and Why:** Coming from our distinctions, write down what is Not Working and why. Complete the table as rows (left to right) rather than as columns (up to down), allowing you to go deep on each area of life before moving on.
3. **Action:** This section holds you accountable for taking action and reducing self-sabotage. When declaring an action, create a small and manageable step that you can **complete**. Completing things is important to build the muscle for follow through.

Area of life	Score (/10)	What's not working?	Why isn't it working? What am I avoiding?	What specific, measurable action can I take to restore workability?
Money	2	No job or revenue with the business. Getting money from partner and parents for rent right now.	What do I need to do, to create money right now? Get a job. Stop overcomplicating the situation and making myself wrong for it.	Spend 30 minutes a day on accounting to know how I am really doing financially. Look through my last monthly expenses and cancel any nonessential subscriptions.

Area of life	Score (/10)	What's not working?	Why isn't it working? What am I avoiding?	What specific, measurable action can I take to restore workability?
Health	4	Have not exercised for 125 days. Eating chips at least four times a week. Gained 10.5 pounds since COVID.	The reasons I tell myself I am failing: (i) No accountability buddy, (ii) Losing my trainer, (iii) No exercise equipment. I am too hard on myself (high expectations).	Complete 30 squats, right after I wake up. Repeat this habit for 30 consecutive days.
Career	4	No job offers or contracts in the last six months. The industry has laid off 80% of workers because of COVID.	Hoping that things will get better on their own. Feeling guilty for being salesy about my services. My partner is taking on the burden of our expenses.	Spend 30 minutes a day saving job postings. Talk to one friend each day, asking for opportunities or employers that they can introduce me to.
Friends	6	Last time I hung out with a friend was 77 days ago. Not being invited to events that friends are hosting.	I deleted social media. I haven't initiated conversations with my friends, yet I am expecting them to. I haven't told my friends that I miss them.	Call one friend each day, and ask them how they are doing. Join three Discord groups to meet and make new friends.

WHEN THINGS WORK

In completing this first section of the book, #REALTALK with Me, we become aware of where we have settled for less than what are capable of in life. We can become (or already are) powerful and intelligent leaders, yet we maintain relationships and workplaces that are tolerable at best.

In understanding workability, we have the tools needed to restore our individual performance. It means holding high standards for ourselves as leaders of leaders, knowing when to quit, and using real talk in order to make our lives workable again.

In being real with ourselves, an opening occurs. We have taken responsibility for our results and our lives so that we can move from passive to active leadership. It is this clear sense of self-leadership that will be our springboard into engaging with others.

We begin to wonder, *What could we create, if we were real with each other?*

PART II

THE SECOND CONVERSATION

#REALTALK with You

The second part, or Conversation, is having real conversations with **others,** especially with your closest and most important people: your co-founders, your investors, and your family. In a report by *Funders and Founders*, 62% of startups fail due to co-founder conflict, which increases with more co-founders.[1] Examples of co-founder conflict include:

- Arguing about whose idea is better
- Deciding who gets what compensation
- Claiming they work harder
- Insisting on strategy rather than execution
- Having different expectations of work-life balance

This Conversation with others addresses the **Heart (Emotions).** When we lie or pretend in front of others, our emotions become suppressed and our words lose power. What you say, claim, or promise has limited value because what needs to be said is hidden away. This tendency to hide amplifies martyrdom and creates an environment of leaders, who act as lone wolves. Every person is for themselves, with no potential for healing, mentorship, or co-creation with the individuals who want you and your organization to succeed. This type of leadership is unhealthy and a wasteful use of resources.

In the entrepreneurial world, a popular support structure is called a **mastermind**, where peers come together in a confidential group to share and solve each other's problems. This term comes from Napoleon Hill's book *Think and Grow Rich*, studying 500 self-made millionaires like Andrew Carnegie and Henry Ford.[2] Hill described a mastermind as, "The coordination of knowledge and effort between two or more people, who work toward a definite purpose in a spirit of harmony."

This collective wisdom is dependent on sharing actual problems by being real and vulnerable, rather than hiding. Allowing ourselves to see and be seen, even in our darker moments, is the inspiration of the #REALTALK movement: leaders of leaders supporting our own.

CHAPTER SIX

AWARENESS

It was October 2018 and I was experiencing an existential crisis.

Two months had passed since my first birthday without Keane. My mother had finished her cancer treatment, which included two major surgeries and many sessions of radiation and chemotherapy.

Being my mum's main caregiver, I was thinking about mortality. I would spend hours with her in the hospital, watching as she sat and received chemo through her veins. Chemo is an intense drug treatment that kills cancer cells while damaging healthy cells.

In undergoing chemo, her appearance changed.

Prior to my mother's diagnosis, she considered herself healthy and youthful. She never dyed her hair before, which was a beautiful jet-black color. My mother was an educator, and at the school where she taught, students and parents thought she was 10 to 20 years younger than her age.

Now, she looked like a completely different person. Her hair was gone, falling away from chemo. She was so pale after treatment and she lost significant weight. She was thinner than I had ever seen her.

Seeing my mum in her most vulnerable state, we got closer than ever before. We talked about life, death, and love. I learned so much about my parents' upbringing and the things she wanted me to remember.

Most of all, I became aware of a new feeling: hope.

I had spent several months being overwhelmed, like a boat being thrashed by the sea. Grief brought so many feelings to the surface and it felt confusing. I had spent decades in survival mode, strategizing and pushing through life's obstacles. It caused me to compartmentalize my feelings by focusing on doing rather than being.

It caused me to disconnect from my body.

In those moments at my mum's bedside, I felt my heart open up. The tenderness of what I experienced and lived through. To talk with her about my childhood and to give myself the space to grieve. To grieve for the childhood I wanted, free of intergenerational trauma and pain. To grieve about the future I lost, with Keane by my side as siblings.

What was possible, now that I was aware of these feelings?

BEING THE STRONGEST

At #REALTALK, we talk a lot about grief. It appears regularly in the spaces we hold for tech founders and investors. Grief is a natural, universal part of being human. It mirrors nature's cycles of life and death, of creation and then destruction.

As we age and pass through life's milestones, grief will be inevitable.

Many of life's greatest moments, and even people, are there for a time. Just a moment in time. This truth occurs not just in the personal arena, but in the professional one too. In holding space for many leaders through #REALTALK, I know this to be true. Grief is the mourning of any significant loss, such as the loss of a co-founder, the letting go of a company's mission, and more.

When Keane died, I felt adrift – lost at sea. For anyone who has lost a loved one, grief is hard to describe in words, yet easy to see in another person's eyes. There is a gravitas, a lived experience, and a quiet wisdom that comes with grief, which cannot be faked. Grief can feel intense and unpredictable, a gauntlet of emotions from rage to sadness to joy.

As leaders of leaders and even trauma survivors, many of us have survived and "succeeded" in life by being strong. This is especially the case in traditional or male-dominated industries like tech, finance, and law, where there are taboos on expressing your emotions or asking for help. I know to compensate for my traumatic childhood, I became "strong." I took care of myself. I became my own champion. I worked hard and hustled, pushing my way to the top.

The path of pure willpower, of pure hustle, worked . . . until it didn't.

Being the strongest, the one who always leads, is a double-edged sword: it is both a blessing and a curse. It creates leaders that are high-functioning and scrappy, but have difficulties in trusting and delegating to others. It creates a feeling of constant pressure and loneliness, unable to take your foot off the pedal. It creates sleepless nights and mistrust, discontent by what success has cost us, personally and professionally, to stay at the top.

In the tales of "hustle and grind," we forget that lone wolves pay the ultimate cost: being lonely at the end of the finish line. A loneliness that can span from months to even decades at a time. In our pursuit to move forward and lead, we can forget to pause, to create the space for feeling, and to allow our humanity to breathe.

In working with CEOs, we have a saying, "What got you here won't get you to the next level." This is especially true when you have become successful by pushing and pushing, often by yourself. However, when we take on massive amounts of responsibility and are leading entire teams or organizations, doing things alone won't cut it. It might be tolerable in the short term, but never in the long run.

The idea of feeling, of allowing emotions in, can seem dangerous to founders and to leaders of leaders. It can feel like removing the armor that got us here – exposed and raw. We want to cover our chests and protect our hearts from future harm or pain. This tendency is especially true in modern times, where we are dealing with enormous stress and a lack of resources. In a scarcity mindset, we may be seeing everything and everyone as a threat.

In my work, I sit with tech founders and business leaders who are in deep amounts of pain. They have the accolades and the money but feel exhausted and resentful of their work. They feel like every day is a slog, a battle, with no reprieve in sight. What is more concerning is that when there are opportunities for rest and recovery, they cannot enjoy them because they are always "on," hyper-vigilant and unable to entrust their work to others.

In this chapter, we begin to take a look at our feelings. We start the journey of unraveling, of unlearning our addiction to hardship and loneliness, opening up a better way to lead. A way to lead with others, so that we aren't doing things alone.

THE WILLINGNESS TO FEEL

When grief entered my life, so did my resistance to feeling.

It was puzzling and impressive at the same time. After spending decades surviving by pushing things down, all of it was coming back up. My coping mechanisms, which were what got me here, were clever and stubborn too.

Every time I tried to approach a feeling, especially one from my adverse childhood, I could feel my body shutting down. My thoughts would drift into nostalgia or daydreaming rather than being present with myself or others. Old habits would appear, like junk food, excessive music, or constant

TV to avoid anything about feeling. These habits felt like a heavy blanket, numbing my pain and, subsequently, my ability to feel anything at all.

The problem is that all healing and all relationships, including the collaborative ones in the workplace, start with our *willingness* to feel.

This word is intentional. We don't have to be ready (and there is no such thing as being 100% ready), but we do have to be willing – to wake up each day and make the choice to feel.

It is in feeling that we begin to restore our relationship with and trust in others.

In understanding feeling, I have seen how it has healed lives, from the individual to the many. In understanding numbing, I have seen how it has destroyed families, teams, and entire communities.

In my own journey, I struggled for many years to understand and accept my own emotions. Growing up in a traditional household, East Asian culture is one of "saving face," of not feeling or showing weakness. It meant that acts of emotion like crying were considered taboo, foreign even. For so many years, I had been unable to cry because I spent so long numbing out my feelings by pushing them down.

It took me many years, in working with therapists, coaches, and mentors, to restore my full range of feeling and the emotions that came with it.

Having spaces to feel is important, but we don't do it enough.

At #REALTALK, most of our clients are leaders (especially men) who have spent decades hiding and numbing their feelings with work, food, alcohol, and sex. The usual vices in high-performing industries like tech, finance, and law.

When we avoid, when we numb out, our sensitivity and awareness of feeling begin to disappear. We lose the capacity to cry, to laugh, and to move our emotions through our bodies. When we bottle our emotions, we lose our ability to lead with clarity and ease. In that world, every day feels heavy or even empty, like a soldier bracing for war.

In my own recovery around feeling, I started where I could.

I joined a grief recovery group five minutes from my house called GriefShare, a global network of volunteers spanning 12 countries. GriefShare is a 13-week program with modules created by subject experts and a curriculum that is delivered by facilitators who have experienced grief themselves. The facilitators have completed the GriefShare program as participants, coming back to help others.

It was in these weekly meetings that I learned it was okay to feel. I was surrounded by individuals that were much older than myself, who had lost so many people but still had the hope and the determination to live. I was receiving support rather than giving and caretaking, allowing someone else to lead. I was creating the space to sit with and process my emotions so that I could slowly but surely move on from Keane's death.

In sharing with them, even in the many sessions where I would cry or get angry, they taught me a lot about my own emotions. That emotions don't have to be a thing to fix, but that simply allowing yourself to feel those emotions was enough. In sharing honestly and earnestly, I felt a release afterwards: a witnessing and a knowing that I would be okay eventually, even if it wasn't in that moment.

It showed me that we as humans (and as leaders) are more similar than we think, and that we don't have to do things alone. In being surrounded by people who were willing to feel, this co-created space became my safe haven. It was a place where I could rest and recover so that I could come back powerfully as a leader of leaders.

WHAT #REALTALK WITH YOU IS ALL ABOUT

In the previous part or Conversation (#REALTALK with Me), we learned that we communicate ineffectively with ourselves, leading to breakdowns in stability, integrity, and/or workability. In schools, in homes, and in the media, we are given unhealthy examples of what it means to use words and to follow through with sincere action. We fight, we argue, we escalate, we accuse, and we deny our responsibility and involvement in our own lives.

With avoidance, we create a world that doesn't work. It is a world that lacks both functionality and performance in multiple areas of our personal and professional lives.

In #REALTALK with You, the next three chapters of this book, we build on this foundation by focusing on the heart. Now that we have taken responsibility for our individual lives, how are we showing up for those around us? How are we leading as leaders of leaders?

Transformation becomes tangible in the public arena, not the private.

When I started #REALTALK five years ago, I came from the world of trauma-informed practice. I was an award-winning teacher in the field of special education with two degrees based in social and developmental psychology. My specialty was students who experienced mental illness and trauma.

In this work, I noticed the inexplicable difference between healing that happened in private versus in public, where students expressed their feelings and their stories in front of others.

The most memorable moment was one afternoon, when one of my students started talking about her experiences with medication. All of the students in that study group had been diagnosed with depression or anxiety at some point and it was like an unspoken secret. She was curious about the learnings her classmates could bring to the table and wondered why they hadn't talked about their experiences with medication before.

Despite my worry – fearing that she had "gone too far" – I was fascinated to learn that the other students were relieved. They loved her shares and the questions she asked. She asked in such a respectful and empowering way, leading the conversation first with her disclosure. They felt relieved to be seen and heard. It was refreshing to know that other people had the same experiences. Instead of keeping that elephant in the room, they decided to create a bridge and to walk across it together.

They began to share their experiences on mental health, and in those shares, they could finally breathe. For the first time, they didn't have to pretend.

In #REALTALK with You, we explore how healing (and our restoration of power) involves others. That many of our traumas were formed from past, unpleasant experiences with parents, friends, coworkers, and more. It means unlearning and even healing the wounds we have acquired, so that we can start fresh without carrying our baggage into the next part of our lives.

As leaders who hold positions of power, we also have undue influence on other people. It is this reality that has created conversations like #MeToo and Black Lives Matter, in an attempt to acknowledge past hurt and to reconcile wrongs.

In our ability to lead, we also have the ability to heal. To be a demonstration for showing up and leading *with* others, even when we don't want to.

That is the mark of a true leader.

WHY AWARENESS MATTERS

In this part, we start our healing journey through awareness. Like the way we cannot solve a problem without knowing it, we cannot embrace our feelings without acknowledging them.

For tech founders, this concept can feel confusing. Most examples of startup unicorns come with stories of 100-hour workweeks and sacrificing relationships, family, and health to make it. Many leaders, especially those who have resisted self-work, will see feelings as a risk factor.

Feelings are only a risk when our relationship with feelings is damaged.

Sadness does not break people. Anger does not break people. But our avoidance of those feelings does. That avoidance leads to self-destruction and self-sabotage in an effort to run away from ourselves and others.

In avoidance, we begin to dim our ability and sensitivity to situations because we aren't paying attention. We become less adaptive in the moment, developing fragility in our leadership. This fragility causes us to lash out and to avoid feedback, rather than ride out the messiness of entrepreneurship. Furthermore, problems and challenges that start out small and even manageable can snowball tremendously without our ability to feel.

In numbing out, we can become our worst enemy and saboteur.

Instead of experiencing our leadership as Control (Cope), awareness begins to shift us toward Calm (Thrive). We begin to see that emotions are comfortable, conversations are routine, and relationships are meaningful. Leadership goes from responding in the moment to managing people and culture. We open up more capacity for ourselves as leaders so that we can focus on the things that matter. For many leaders, it means not just working *in* the business, but working *on* the business by carving out the space and time to strategize for the future.

This piece is key in not just entering the game of innovation but actually competing in it. We cannot innovate by just doing what we've always done; we will need to tap into new stores of capacity, so we can design and execute on solutions for the future of the organization. We need this capacity in training the next generation of leaders as well, who can help carry this burden alongside us.

Great things are never done alone, and every person who has been successful at a large scale has always had a team of employees, partners, or supporters to help them along the way.

Awareness is the first step in prevention, rather than reaction. Rather than being bystanders and enablers, we become leaders in our workplaces and in our homes. Emotional awareness has tangible benefits to doing business. Research by Embroker, a leading business insurance provider, found that co-founder conflict is an inevitable and detrimental part of startups:[1]

- Forty-three percent of founders split up because of internal arguments
- Seventy-one percent of conflicts are due to differences in the company's direction
- Eighteen percent feel the ousted co-founder didn't share the company's values

When we embark on large goals or complex problems, especially in the game of innovation, we will enter situations that are emotionally charged. People will have differing ways to handle their stress and differing ways they want to be supported. Thus, awareness is key in seeing and preventing interpersonal problems in the workplace before it is too late.

A CAUTIONARY TALE ABOUT BURNOUT

In order to bring awareness into your life, there is a caveat. As leaders of leaders, it is important for us to manage **burnout**, the numbing out of feelings and physical, mental, and emotional exhaustion that occurs from overwork. I talk about burnout because it has become a commonplace yet underestimated problem in organizations large and small.

In the early days of #REALTALK, I used to host confidential CEO circles at existing tech conferences. I remember the first #REALTALK Circle I hosted. I was sitting in an open field at an outdoor conference with 1000 attendees on-site, and 40 of those people (all CEOs) had attended my circle. I remember opening up the circle, setting the parameters for how we would engage each other and sharing my own story on mental health, so that others could feel free to do the same.

What was peculiar for me back then was the number of founders I met who were burnt out. So burnt out that they couldn't tell what was up from now. They were so overworked that their body and even their minds were numbed out. I remember being approached by these founders after I was alone, in order to ask me questions like, "How do you know if you're burnt out? How do you know if you're sad? How can you tell when you need to rest?"

The fact that they were asking such foundational questions, which they couldn't answer themselves, was emblematic of the lack of awareness in the workplace.

As you continue this journey, use the practices from the previous chapters to restore and maintain your baseline level of self-care. If we as leaders of leaders continue to burn out and to fill every pocket of time with work, there is never space to acknowledge, process, and release our emotions. There is never an opportunity to take a breath and to recover; there is only an unsustainable lifestyle of checking off the next thing.

Awareness requires us to create the space for emotions to surface, so that we can process them.

THE POWER OF LABELING

At #REALTALK, our use of language is precise. The precision of that language transforms a space and the way that people relate to others and their experiences. In my story about GriefShare, the relief came from knowing that my experience (the loss of my only sibling) had a name. It meant that I wasn't "crazy, broken, or too much."

I was no longer alone. I had resources and people who could help.

In my line of work, we call this action **labeling**. By identifying something for what it is, we take away the fear of the unknown. When we face uncertainty, our minds can conjure vivid images of the worst. These images are rarely real, like the difference between Fear versus Danger.

Yet these what-ifs can cause us significant emotional burden, leading to anxiety.

In Chapter Two, we talked about cognitive biases, which dilute our ability to see things (and thus, label things) as they really are. Examples such as Attribute Substitution and the Availability Heuristic affect our memories, our thoughts, and the stories we convey.

In Workability, you learned how to remove story and drama from the way you communicate about problems. In Awareness, we extend this practice toward emotions. We learn how to label an emotion for what it is so that we can process and release it.

When I teach this work to those who are new to emotions, it is akin to a paint palette. Imagine our emotions as different colors, each with different tints. What are emotions (e.g. red, yellow, blue) that exist within you? Furthermore, what are the variations within that emotion? For example, maroon, burgundy, and cherry are forms of red with subtle differences.

When we label something for what it is, we can heal it. We can communicate it. We can bring it into a shared space with another person to get the support and help we need.

On the other hand, when we label something incorrectly, it can cause mayhem and suffering. In experiences of divorce and grief, mislabeling can destroy rather than heal. In a 2006 study by The Compassionate Friends, an organization that supports bereaved parents, it was found that 16% of couples divorce after the loss of a child.[2]

When my parents lost Keane, it brought up so many uncomfortable and intense emotions for us as a family. I cannot imagine what it is like to lose a child, to know that you outlived them and wondering what their life could have been. How were they going to navigate life now, knowing that this loss was irreversible?

In the early months of loss, many marriages fall into fighting, blaming, and numbing out. It can be scary to comprehend, much less process these emotions. In the instance of Keane's passing, it took us years to move from denial to anger to acceptance. The acceptance meant acknowledging that Keane passed away and that we needed to let go of blame to move on.

Correct labeling could alleviate the suffering experienced in these immensely stressful moments. For instance, rather than labeling something as, "It's your fault this happened" (Blame), other labels that could be used are:

- "I don't know how to process all this pain." (Despair)
- "I'm so angry that my child's life was cut short." (Rage)
- "I'm glad they knew how much I loved them." (Gratitude)

These labels allow us to process emotions in a healthy way so that we can process loss and other major stressors in the personal and professional realm.

Labeling an emotion allows us to move through that emotion. It stops us from entering a rabbit hole, which is common in depression, where individuals sink deeper into the darkness. It breaks the pattern of complaining and blaming by taking responsibility and action. It creates a third-party observer, pointing to an emotion and saying, "Oh, that's what it is. It explains a lot!"

You cannot solve a problem unless you know what it is. Labeling gets us unstuck.

Given the importance of labeling, how do we build this muscle?

INTERNAL EXERCISE: THE COLOR PALETTE

When I taught special education as a K–8 teacher, I worked with students on the Autism Spectrum and others who had Down Syndrome. A powerful tool we used was called augmentative and alternative communication (AAC).

For neurotypical leaders, we take our innate communication skills for granted. Those who are neurodiverse may process and label social information, such as emotions and nuances like sarcasm, differently. AAC uses pictures to facilitate nonverbal communication, in order to demystify the relationship between an experience and its label.[3] For example, the word "not" is symbolized with a picture of an X, so that the word and its nonverbal (visual) expression are associated with one another. It makes communication clearer.

How does this relate to you as a leader of leaders? When we are emotionally blocked, we become disconnected from and even confused by our own thoughts, emotions, and actions. To restore real talk in our lives, we need to understand what we are feeling and how to describe it. By directing our attention to our internal experience, we can become reacquainted with which emotions we are experiencing at different moments.

Instructions:

1. Imagine your emotions are like a Pantone Color Chart, where we can see all the shades and variations of a single color like red. Emotions are the same way. At first, you may only know the general color (red). However, as you practice labeling in real time, this precision will increase and allow you to unlock nuance in your emotions (maroon). This exercise strengthens your connection to the Emotion Wheel, the eight major categories of emotions as described by psychologist Robert Plutchik in the 1980s.[4]

2. Carry a small notebook and a set of markers. Each day, you will open up a new page in your notebook. As you experience your day from the time you wake up, be aware of the emotions you experience. As you feel a certain category of emotions (e.g. red for anger, yellow for joy), take a related marker and draw a colored dot. Continue to do this for each emotion that you experience until you fall asleep.

3. Jot down these emotions for a week.

Reflection: Once you have seven days' worth of Emotional Pages, let's reflect.

1. **Daily:** How many emotions did you experience each day? Calculate your Daily Totals and then your Weekly Total.

2. **Weekly:** Look at your Daily and Weekly Totals. Do they surprise you? Which day had the lowest number? Which day had the highest? What are you noticing about your emotions?

3. **Frequency:** Tally each category of emotions for a Color Total. Which color had the lowest number? Which color had the highest? What can you conclude about yourself?

4. **Difficulty:** What was it like, identifying your emotions this week? Was it easy or difficult? Did you encounter resistance or confusion, and if so, what was it?

5. **Pattern:** What patterns are you seeing? What triggers or associations come up for each emotion? For example, yellow (Joy) is associated with your best friend and blue (Sadness) comes up when you're alone at night.

EXTERNAL EXERCISE: HOW ARE YOU REALLY DOING?

In this next exercise, we extend our awareness by expressing our emotions in real time. In declaring our emotions aloud, we begin the practice of taking responsibility for our lives. Remember that the vehicle for real talk is language.

In being precise with the way we think, listen, and speak, we can become leaders and not followers in our lives and in the workplace.

Instructions:

1. **Connection:** Much of our life involves interactions with others. Humans are a tribal species meant to be in a community with one another. One of the most common questions we get asked is, "How are you doing?" You will build on this question by asking the people you encounter in your day, "How are you *really* doing?" This additional word makes all the difference.

2. **Honesty:** You will conduct at least three of these conversations each day for a week. In asking this question, people will become more honest about their feelings. It will give you an opportunity to be honest about yours in turn.

3. **Feeling:** When you share your feelings, use the following sentence to start: "I feel _____." Do not worry about the why behind these emotions. Just focus on the experience of it. How would you describe the feeling with adjectives or visuals? We often focus on the "why" (Past) to avoid feeling.

4. **Curiosity:** Notice what happens in the conversation. What did that person share with you? What surprised or moved you about these interactions?

5. **Bonus:** Consider having a conversation with these groups of people:

   - **Resistant:** There are people in our lives who we avoid, resent, or are annoyed with. When was the last time you listened from a place of non-judgment? Note that curiosity is not the same as care or commitment. Being curious is taking an observer role, while maintaining discernment and boundaries where necessary.
   - **Distant:** There are others (like friends and family) who we were close to and have lost touch with. This is especially true with the rise of remote work. Reach out to people who you are wondering about. How is your childhood friend doing? How about that colleague from your previous workplace? Allow yourself to experiment!

ANSWERING THE CALL

As high performers, we need to treat our mental and emotional health as seriously as our work. Like athletes, leaders of leaders are required to perform at a moment's notice, navigating crises or obstacles on a daily basis. In a messy world of uncertainty and change, the importance of our mental and emotional health cannot be understated.

In starting your journey with emotions, you begin to develop resiliency rather than fragility in your leadership. It means being able to handle higher amounts of real talk, not just with yourself but with others, so that you can adapt in real time. It means moving from reaction to prevention, so that we can solve problems while they are small. It means being able to depend on your team, your friends, and your family rather than operating as a lone wolf. In the next chapter, we will build on this understanding by cultivating your emotional mastery.

CHAPTER SEVEN

COMPASSION

It was December 2018 and the first anniversary was coming. The first anniversary of Keane's death.

Through GriefShare, I was no longer avoiding, suppressing, or judging my emotions. It felt safe to be in rooms with people who had the capacity to hold space for my shares. Unlike the numerous responsibilities I bore in childhood, where I was taking care of others, GriefShare felt different.

In being with others who were experiencing grief, I received permission. Permission to be with my emotions.

What started as an opening, like the cracking open of a door, became something more. Once my heart started to feel, it became a flood.

Other emotions started to appear, like rage and resentment, and my life started to heal. It was healing because I was acknowledging and processing emotions I had been avoiding for so long. It felt like a weight off of my shoulders, as I confronted the wounds underneath those emotions and the experiences I needed to make peace with.

I was also getting media attention for my work with #REALTALK, being commended by other leaders in the tech industry. I was excelling professionally and we were helping thousands of founders. Even though I missed Keane, I created something meaningful from this loss.

#REALTALK was my salvation, a way to process what happened.

The truth was: I used entrepreneurship to deal with my trauma. Every company I had built or invested in reflected the journey within myself. When I was struggling with mental illness, I created a tutoring company that served gifted and neurodiverse students. When I was struggling with the years lost to abuse, I invested in our blockchain company to "fight for the bottom billion." When I was struggling with Keane's death, I created #REALTALK to bring tough conversations into the open.

It was in #REALTALK, witnessing the tenderness and humanity of other founders, that I found myself again.

A more human Cherry Rose. The Cherry Rose that I remembered and embraced emotions like sadness, anger, and joy. The Cherry Rose who wrote poetry every day and danced in random places for fun. This Cherry Rose was willing to experiment and to trust that things would be okay.

It was in these moments that I realized how many years I lost to numbing out, to pretending, and to being perfect. There was something so dear and precious in reconnecting with my human, the more messy, and yet authentic side to who I was as a person and as a leader of leaders.

I decided that my experience was perfectly human. I was trying each and every day to be a little better, a newfound kindness to how I treated myself. I was giving myself the space and the resources to process and heal and I was willing to listen. I was asking for the help I needed and had an incredible team of professionals and mentors alongside me.

I was being compassionate with myself. I was putting myself first.

THE WORLD OF EMOTIONS

To understand compassion, we must first understand how emotions impact results.

Dr. David R. Hawkins, a renowned physician and psychiatrist, was one of the pioneers in the field of consciousness research. In studying his patients, he noticed that certain emotions had specific effects on his patients – physiological responses that could be measured. Hawkins began to label, describe, and measure emotions and their effects on the body, in hopes of maximizing physical, mental, and emotional performance.

What he found was groundbreaking.

In his 1995 book *Power vs. Force*, he postulated the Map of Consciousness, a way to sort lower versus higher consciousness and their related emotions.[1] Emotions of lower consciousness were Force (push), requiring effort and struggle to get by. Emotions of higher consciousness were Power (pull), maximizing situations and opportunities to support you.

There was no such thing as "wrong" emotions, only differences in outcome.

Furthermore, he noticed a turning point in consciousness, where emotions shift from force to power. When individuals embody the emotion of Courage, they take responsibility for their lives and their identity shifts from victim to leader. Courage is the choice to act rather than avoid or blame. Courage is the starting point of power.

In hearing about these findings, you might be asking, *Why does this matter?*

In the game of business and innovation, most leaders operate from Force. According to the #REALTALK Leadership model, leaders are focused on Control (Cope) by doing and managing as much as they can. Oftentimes, this "doing" occurs by being a lone wolf and working long hours, leading to excessive burnout and leaders who are unable to delegate or be supported by their teams, their mentors, and even their friends and family. In a pervasive culture of hustle-and-grind where we are "not enough," it becomes the breeding ground for shame and stigma. When we are surrounded by communities and media that are selling a false story that everyone's got their stuff together, it breeds emotions of lower consciousness. Emotions like fear and grief become present in every interaction, and leaders begin to hide.

Leaders play the game. They smile and say they're okay when they really aren't.

The implications are severe because over time, it is impossible for any leader, no matter how high performing they are, to do things alone. This is especially true when facing the largest and most exponential technologies of the century. The pace in which we are experiencing change is not one that leaders can or should pursue alone. Our ability to rise to the occasion and to compete in the game of innovation will require us to become a **leader of leaders:** not just being leaders ourselves, but transforming the individuals around us into leaders too. When we create leaders around us, they free up our capacity at a team or organizational level, so that we can sustain our performance for longer and at a higher quality.

In my work with #REALTALK, I coached Diversity, Equity, and Inclusion and Mental Health leaders who were burnt out personally and professionally. Most of these leaders became exhausted after a career of fighting and advocacy. I share this observation because even the most mission-driven of organizations will exhaust and eventually fail, if we are unable to build teams that we can trust and depend on. Operating from Force in the long run is unsustainable, and it is a miserable lifestyle with serious costs like our physical health and our family relationships.

How can you fill the cups of others when your own is empty? You can't.

OUR RELATIONSHIP WITH SHAME

In stepping into Power, we must address our relationship with Shame. In the dictionary, **shame** is defined as "a painful emotion caused by having done something wrong or improper." It is the number one emotion we address at #REALTALK because self-destructive behavior feeds the stigma of mental health. When we experience stigma in any space, it evokes related emotions like fear and anger and it reduces the potential for any solutions to surface.

After all, how can we create solutions when we aren't willing to talk about the problem? When we are stuck in the shame, in blaming ourselves for "being or doing wrong"?

When we look at the workplace as a whole, there have been many leaders who sit back or even enable silence as they and others struggle with mental illness and trauma. I imagine a big part of this shame is not due to ill intent, but because of the shame around their own struggles.

In the world of #REALTALK, I saw this on a regular basis. I would travel from city to city, hosting these confidential CEO circles, and it would take so much care and planning to even get sharing from folks. There were folks who had been in the industry for decades, hiding in plain sight. They would share in our #REALTALK Circles and eventually our #REALTALK Masterminds (a long-form version of our one-time circles), only to continue pretending at work, in their homes, and more.

This culture of pretending was prevalent with the people who enabled Tony Hsieh's drug use prior to his death. Hsieh was surrounded by so many people, yet he felt unable to ask for help. Shame is an incredibly heavy emotion, and in making ourselves wrong, we become a former shell of ourselves and who we can be.

The fact is: shame is a strong and compelling force, and by processing this emotion, we can create a turning point in someone's life. Why is that?

In *Power vs. Force*, the "lowest" of all emotions is shame. Shame is the most destructive emotion that exists because it is self-hate: destruction toward the self. In a world where tech founders and leaders of leaders are stressed and dealing with internal and external crises, adding shame is lethal.

The game of business and innovation comes with specific rules, said and unsaid, and its players are not meant to navigate the world alone. It is why in the world of startups, we have clearly defined ecosystems and supports like accelerators, VC firms, and more. These supports appear at the very beginning of a tech founder's journey and rightly so. When we introduce these supports early and protect our founders, like the way a mother bird protects and feeds her baby, they have a better fighting chance. They have a chance to survive and to get the mentorship they need from other leaders, so by the time they need to leave the nest, they are as ready as one can be.

In choosing to operate alone as leaders, we risk breakdowns in our mental, emotional, or physical health. We risk breakdowns in our ability to lead our teams as well, and to maximize the power of our relationships and the people around us.

Unfortunately, it is when leaders need the most help that they choose to hide and pretend.

Shame is incredibly common in the workplace. It is linked with **imposter syndrome**, where we feel like frauds despite our accomplishments and qualifications. It is linked with **stigma**, where we carry fear and even discrimination against mental illness and trauma. It is linked with the tech industry and other high-performing industries where we are so rich in money, yet so bankrupt in our mental and emotional disposition.

Mental illness, trauma, sexism, and racism. These issues have run rampant in the workplace because we avoid real talk. We avoid looking into the mirror and taking responsibility. We preach wokeness, where we say that mental health is important, yet continue to stay on the sidelines.

That is no way to lead.

In stepping into #REALTALK, we must let go of any shame with ourselves and others. We must create the space for an empowering type of leadership.

ACKNOWLEDGING MEN'S MENTAL HEALTH

Before I go further in this chapter, I want to talk about men's mental health. When I led #REALTALK, many of our clients were men because of our focus on the tech industry. As of 2023, global equity management platform Carta reported that only 13.2% of tech founders were women or nonbinary, meaning that 86.8% of tech founders are men.[2] In the past several years, men have also outnumbered women when it comes to new tech founders by a ratio of six to one.

If you are a man reading this book, there are additional considerations you may be grappling with. Men in general have been socialized with phrases like "boys don't cry" and have spent decades in a societal culture that hasn't supported or encouraged them to be vulnerable. And in some instances, when men have chosen to be vulnerable by disclosing that they need help, it has been received with mixed reception or even emasculation.

In leaning into the "real" in real talk, here is some important context in understanding the mental health landscape and struggles of men. In 2021, CBC News published an in-depth report on men's mental health in Canada and discovered that:[3]

- Men represent more than 75% of suicides, accounting for an average of 50 deaths per week by suicide.
- Men are three times more likely to experience addiction and substance abuse (e.g. alcohol, cannabis, opioids) compared to women.
- In the province of British Columbia, men accounted for 81% of deaths by drug overdose.
- Men aged 18–34 report a 63% rate for "considerable loneliness and isolation," compared to 53% of women in the same age bracket.

Men's mental health is not talked about enough, where men often choose not to share or disclose at all. When they do struggle with mental health, many of them self-medicate with substances rather than building ties with others and asking for help. This has grave implications on not just the personal lives of men but in how these dynamics affect the workplace.

Speaking from experience, #REALTALK came on to the scene and resonated with so many leaders (especially men) because we have come to a point where hiding, avoiding, and numbing are no longer bearable coping mechanisms in the workplace. In a fast-paced world where performing poorly may mean losing your job or your company going bankrupt, the stakes are higher than ever to take care of ourselves before we reach breakdown.

Aside from these stats, there are comparable ones in other parts of the world like Europe. A comprehensive study done by Priory, the leading provider of mental healthcare in the United Kingdom, surveyed 1000 men and discovered that:[4]

- Seventy-seven percent of men have experienced mental health conditions like anxiety or depression.
- Forty percent of men have never spoken to anyone about their mental health.
- Twenty-nine percent say they are "too embarrassed" to talk about their mental health, while 20% say there is a "negative stigma."
- The biggest stressors for men are their work (32%), their finances (31%), and their health (23%).
- Forty percent of men said it would take thoughts of suicide or self-harm to convince them to get professional help.

Thus, when we speak about shame and the importance of healing our relationship with emotions, I hope that you are gentle with yourself. If you are a man reading this or a leader with men on your team, take this social context into consideration. We must acknowledge that each of us, given

our cultural, racial, socioeconomic, and gender identity, will have a different relationship and even definition of mental health. Some people will
have grown up in circles where sharing and connection are common and
even encouraged, and others where they were considered taboo.

In later chapters, we will cover best practices and diversity, equity, and
inclusion (DEI), in order to better support the different folks in our lives
who are struggling with burnout, stress, or mental health.

THE CYCLES
OF DISEMPOWERMENT

To break free of shame and the resistance to share, we have to understand
our patterns. As humans, we adopt insidious ways to disempower ourselves and others, many of which are subconscious and unintentional.

In the 1960s, famed psychiatrist Dr. Stephen Karpman created the
Drama Triangle. Like his father, who was a pioneer in criminal psychoa-
nalysis, Karpman derived his findings from his clients who were in dysfunctional families.

The Drama Triangle is a powerful framework for understanding the
consequences of unprocessed trauma or hurt and the unhealthy roles that
we adopt as a result:[5]

1. **Victim (The Helpless):** "Poor me!" The Victim stays in the cycle of
   powerless and stuck, foregoing responsibility to themselves
   and others.
2. **Rescuer (The Martyr):** "Poor you!" The Rescuer is an enabler by
   "saving" everyone else, making others dependent on them.
3. **Persecutor (The Bully):** "It's your fault!" The Persecutor avoids the
   problem altogether by dominating the relationship and blaming
   everyone else.

In looking at the tech industry and other workplaces, many leaders operate from the Drama Triangle. Rather than taking the lead on systemic issues like mental health, we bystand, enable, and even blame.

#REALTALK exists because of a grave need for leaders to step up and take responsibility. To build the emotional stamina and resilience to have tough conversations and to do hard things.

In our earlier days of #REALTALK, we saw employees mistrust founders and founders mistrust investors. Investors spoke of the frustration they had, seeing founders as poor communicators who often withheld or lied. Investors were jumping from crisis to crisis from their founders after problems were disclosed too late. Furthermore, I repeatedly experienced employees who approached me after events to share that their employer "doesn't care about mental health," and that even if their boss wanted to support this, they couldn't because their CEO expects everyone to work late. To work as hard as they can to the expense of everyone's physical and mental health.

I even remember an employee who couldn't leave work until 10:00 p.m. each day because the CEO would stay at the office until that time or even later (sometimes midnight). At that startup, it was unsaid that if you left before the CEO, you were mocked, punished, and shamed for being the "weak link" (e.g. adopting a Persecutor mindset).

In a world where we as leaders operate from the Drama Triangle, we are afraid to empower others. Instead of creating leaders around us, we can become the poison inside teams and organizations, tearing down others and even grinding them down to the point of breakdown. As a result, we operate from Control (Cope), micromanaging and dismissing the potential of those around us.

We put others down in order to rise.

It is hard to be preventive, much less innovative, in a world of Control.

Even in examples like the Rescuer, the dynamic is unhealthy for all parties, as it enables a parasitic (rather than symbiotic) relationship. During COVID-19, Canada saw one of its largest charities, WE Charity (formerly Free the Children), fall into controversy, followed by an organizational hiatus and a governmental investigation. In a report by The Huffington Post, former volunteers were distressed by WE's "voluntourism" model: privileged individuals who tour and "help" poorer countries.[6]

Voluntourists build schools and then leave, creating a paternalistic model common in the world of charity. Rather than breaking the cycle of poverty, these communities become dependent on the organization and leaving them stuck in victimhood. This inequality was further exemplified by the discovery of WE Charity's spending on political and celebrity figures in Canada.

Given this context, how can we move away from the Drama Triangle? It is clear that these roles are unsustainable in the long run, and not a viable path to enduring success. As leaders, how can we cultivate and encourage the self-growth and self-leadership of those around us?

FROM DRAMATIC TO EMPOWERING

Forty years after the creation of Karpman's Drama Triangle, there was a breakthrough in the dialog. David Emerald Womeldorff, a professional facilitator and an executive coach, created a framework to work in parallel with the Drama Triangle called the Empowerment Dynamic. Womeldorff believed that Karpman's research opened a window to the growth-oriented roles that could be created, a positive alternative that leaders could choose based on mindset and action.

Under the Empowerment Dynamic, each Drama role could be transformed into its parallel Empowerment role:[7]

1. **Creator:** "I can do it!" The Victim becomes the Creator, owning their power and creating new outcomes through choices.
2. **Coach:** "How will you do it?" The Rescuer becomes the Coach, supporting others by asking questions and facilitating clarity.
3. **Challenger:** "You can do it!" The Prosecutor becomes the Challenger, calling people forward and evoking action in others.

In seeing our dramatic side and our empowering side, real talk empowers us to embrace our wounds and the wisdom they hold. In choosing the path of facing our demons and acknowledging where we've let down others and even ourselves, we break free.

Rather than numbing and dissociating from our drama, we can acknowledge our wholeness as individuals and as leaders. No saving, no blaming, just witnessing and holding space for someone's humanity.

That, in itself, is enough.

"It is the difference between empathy and compassion," says my colleague, a renowned therapist of nearly 20 years. Specializing in working with survivors of abuse, she taught me a lot about holding space. In **empathy**, we take on someone's pain, feeling the same feelings they are feeling. Empathy is what leads to poor boundaries and then exhaustion as practitioners try to "save" other people.

In **compassion**, we acknowledge and witness someone's pain. Our boundaries are healthy and resolute. We support people by reminding them of their wholeness. We don't do their healing for them, but we empower them as leaders so they have the confidence to do so. Compassion is healing rather than saving, moving away from drama-related emotions like panic, guilt, and shame.

Leadership can be real, kind, and healthy. Compassion is a way forward.

BUILDING YOUR EMOTIONAL STAMINA

To lead during stressful and volatile times, we need to train.

Similar to the way that athletes train for physical stamina, our emotional muscles can be practiced and strengthened. This step is critical because #REALTALK with You is not just leading ourselves but engaging the most important people in our lives, like our spouses and our colleagues.

Since industries like tech are predominantly male, there continues to be ignorance and avoidance of emotional work. Rather than allowing emotions, men are told to "shove your feelings down."

Emotions become a scary place (and rightly so) because there are few healthy examples in the mainstream or in the workplace.

In exercising our emotional muscles, we release these beliefs (many of which are fear, not danger) and move away from the Drama Triangle. Once a pipe filled with emotional gunk, our ability to move through our emotions creates an opening.

It gets us unstuck. It creates a reset, a clearing, so that we can lead powerfully in a situation . . . without all that gunk.

To have emotional stamina, boundaries are a key part of this. In empathy, founders are overly attached by equating their worth or identity to success, relationships, or some external factor requiring validation. In compassion, founders are whole and complete, fully present with others, and exercising healthy boundaries.

They understand what crap is theirs and what to leave on the ground.

Boundaries are essential. From the world of psychology, **boundaries** are the limits between you and another person that dictate what is acceptable versus unacceptable behavior.[8] Without boundaries, founders open themselves up to physical, mental, or emotional risk from others and their environment. They say yes to situations, commitments, or relationships that are inappropriate or ill-suited, causing problems to escalate or snowball.

By knowing your boundaries, psychological safety and permission can be created in any situation. Leadership is restored in the founder, who can communicate what they need. Boundaries and standards go hand-in-hand too because a leader with high standards will practice boundaries as a result. After all, if something does not meet your standard, we are saying no and removing ourselves from that potential drama or commitment.

To bring real talk into our lives, boundaries matter.

In Brené Brown's *Daring Greatly,* she speaks of the difference between vulnerability and oversharing: "Using vulnerability is not the same thing as being vulnerable; it's the opposite—it's armour." Brown notes that speaking and listening without boundaries pushes people away, burdening them with our hardships before we have asked permission or built trust.[9] We have seen this in the social media arena, where people "overshare" or disclose highly triggering things without permission or warning.

Sharing without discernment (similar to the feeling of verbal diarrhea) is exhausting and triggering: an unsustainable form of leadership. As a leader of leaders, it is your responsibility to know who, when, and how to share in a way that empowers. For instance, if your organization is going through a tough time and your direct reports are looking to you to lead, it is *not* their job to be your therapist. The power dynamic is imbalanced, and what would be more appropriate is asking a peer, a friend, or even a mentor to hold space for you instead.

By practicing compassion and allowing ourselves to accept emotions and people as they are, without condoning their behavior, we begin to let go of our past. We become nimbler as business leaders as we leave the emotional and mental baggage on the ground so that we can really create and mobilize in the game of innovation.

Given the importance of compassion in cultivating this well of emotional stamina, how do we practice compassion as leaders?

INTERNAL EXERCISE: HELL YES OR NO

To strengthen our boundaries, we need to acknowledge their current state and restore them. Trauma survivors will especially benefit from this exercise, where their boundaries have eroded over the years. By having boundaries, we can keep our tank full and bring our best selves to every situation.

Language is important because boundaries become real by using the words yes or no. The word "yes" is akin to opening our fence (boundary) and allowing someone into our personal, most intimate space. The word "no" is akin to closing our fence and keeping our life intact, as others stay in their separate spaces.

When we give someone our yes, their words and actions have a greater impact on our lives because we are lifting that boundary. It is like allowing a guest into your physical home who can either contribute or take from you and your loved ones. When we give someone our no, we are exercising our right to boundaries and reaffirming what we value as leaders. This lesson is especially important for leaders who are healing from unhealthy boundaries or parasitic relationships.

What is your relationship to yes and no?

Instructions:

1. **Yes:** Write all the things you say yes to, such as events, responsibilities, and people. Yes means that we have added that action or responsibility on our to-do list, whether it is mental, emotional, or physical. What is taking up space in your life?
2. **No:** Write all the things you say no to. Note: You can only include things that are a definite no. If you're a no to your ex, but you're still seeing them, that is not a no because the commitment is ongoing. Be honest with yourself!

3. **Patterns:** Afterward, compare the two columns. Which column is longer? What are you noticing about yourself? Do your commitments reflect who you are and what you value? Founders who feel exhausted, frustrated, and stuck can expect the Yes column to be longer than the No column.

4. **Alignment:** Take a highlighter. In the Yes column, highlight any item that is **not** a Hell Yes. A Hell Yes is defined as a 100% alignment with who you are and what you value. Usually, leaders say yes to things that are "good enough" or "okay" due to obligation, weakening their boundaries in the long run.

5. **Choices:** Anything that was highlighted now belongs to the No column. For the next week, practice saying no to the highlighted activities and even delegating those responsibilities to others.

6. **Influences:** Based on the patterns you see, who has influenced your beliefs on responsibility? On saying yes or no? Usually, the formation of our boundaries (or lack of) can be traced back to childhood, especially with parents or authority figures.

Yes	No	Patterns: the behaviors that I repeat are . . .	Influences: the experiences that shaped me are . . .
My mother-in-law Coffees with people asking to "pick my brain" Taking care of my mother-in-law Running men's support group Supporting my friend who is depressed	Hangouts with my high school friends Hangouts with my university friends Movie nights My unhealthy ex Working after 8:00 p.m.	I say yes to my parents, even when I don't want to. Being their caregiver is exhausting. I say no to my friends, especially when events are not work related. I lack play and joy in my life. I say yes out of obligation. I am rarely happy or content.	Growing up, my dad was in a toxic relationship with my stepmother, but he was too scared to leave. In witnessing their relationship, he learned to say yes to everything she asked, even if it hurt him. Over a prolonged period, he lost his ability to exercise boundaries and eventually, his sense of self.

EXTERNAL EXERCISE: HOLDING SPACE

Aside from boundaries, we must release our addiction to the Drama Triangle. Being "real" in real talk is not about saving, but about holding space for people to be seen and heard. Through our compassion, people learn that they aren't alone. In mental health, what often kills people is not the mental illness itself but the shame and self-destruction.

These people feel broken or less than human.

Witnessing and holding space can cause transformation by shifting shame into acceptance. At #REALTALK, we are known as the "first step." We work with organizations to create an opening for a deeper conversation about mental health. An opening, a possibility that things could be different, can transform a life.

Instructions:

1. **People:** Choose three people in your life whom you want a deeper connection with. Practice discernment in this selection by excluding people who have or could expose you to serious physical, mental, or emotional harm, such as unhealthy exes.

2. **Paraphrasing:** Spend one week reaching out and speaking with these people. As they share, practice paraphrasing: demonstrating an understanding of the other person by repeating their words back to them. Paraphrasing can be used to appreciate their presence and to verify their shares.

3. **Feedback:** If you are a poor listener, it will show in your results. If people feel misunderstood, give them an opportunity to repeat what they shared. Their shares might look like: "Actually, what I said was . . ." or "Not quite, but . . ."

4. **Observations:** If the person repeats or corrects a share, get curious. What did you add to your paraphrasing that wasn't there? What assumptions or interpretations are you carrying with you? Write those down.

5. **Bonus:** The prompts below can be used to increase understanding, connection, and engagement between you and the other person:

   - What do you mean by that?
   - What is it like to be you?
   - Could you explain it to me in a different way?
   - What else would you like to share with me?

THE CLEARING

In cultivating compassion in how we listen and speak, we move away from Control (Cope) toward Calm (Thrive) as a way of leading. Instead of moments and conversations steeped in drama, we can shift our role to one of empowerment. Creating empowered leaders around us, where we are championing their growth and receiving support from these leaders as a result.

Additionally, our wounds inform how we can best serve and empower others at work and at home. Emotions are no longer a poison but an invitation for deep work and resilient leadership.

With our newfound emotional stamina, we can expand our work into the hardest and most intimate arena of all: the people closest to us, such as our spouses and our colleagues. We can look at our mistakes and make amends where necessary so that we can leave our baggage behind. We can start anew, rejuvenated in mind, heart, and body.

CHAPTER EIGHT

FORGIVENESS

I t was December 2019 and another Christmas was here. A different kind of Christmas.

Just a month ago, I had a long heart-to-heart with my family. We had been through so much after Keane's loss and everyone was getting older – I wanted to have this conversation before it was too late.

If there was a possibility for family healing, I took it. I wanted to put the past behind me, to leave the heaviness and the loss behind. To make sure that we could move forward in our lives without bitterness and regret.

For several days, I had real talk with the family member who had hurt me in childhood. It was confronting and uncomfortable, but we did it. We made space for the elephants in the room, all of the things left unsaid over years of fighting.

Living in the family house after Keane's passing was too much. There was a history there. I was exhausted physically, mentally, and emotionally on a regular basis and it led to anxiety attacks. I couldn't fully grieve for Keane as a sister until I had a space to call my own.

Mirroring the pain I felt long ago, I desired to be cherished. To be taken care of. I needed the space to take care of myself, in order to fill my physical, mental, and emotional cup.

Instead of putting others before myself to the point of martyrdom, I moved out. It was a scary decision to make and one that I grappled with for months, but I knew it was the right thing to do. I needed to put myself first, to embody the lessons I learned from Keane's passing about prioritizing your personal well-being (and what happens when you don't).

I decided to move into a different part of the city, in a high-rise apartment that overlooked all of Toronto. In this new home, I was leaping into the unknown. I had spent years of my childhood in chaos, walking on eggshells and solving other people's problems.

For the first time in my life, I was experiencing quiet in my own home. True quiet. I could hear my thoughts and in being with myself, I began to unravel my armor and the identity that came with it. The identity I had prided myself for so long, of being a fighter and a caregiver.

I had spent so long being the savior of the family, and that role wasn't necessary anymore. I was no longer a sibling entrepreneur either – trying to understand my path without Keane by my side. Both of those roles were no longer healthy for me to maintain and it was time to let go. There was space and freedom to design my chosen future. In building a more loving and gentle relationship with myself, I felt ready to explore these deep and existential questions.

Who is Cherry Rose without the trauma? Who am I?

THE WORLD
OF RESENTMENT

In returning to wholeness, we begin to reconcile our past. As leaders of leaders, our industry can feel like a ruthless and lonely place, a dog-eat-dog world where everyone fends for themselves. In fighting our way to the top, we wear armor and build walls to protect ourselves.

In our need to self-protect, we build up resentment, anger, and frustration over past events and relationships. The path to success has high-highs and low-lows, and no one is immune to things like loss and betrayal in a lifetime. It is this cynicism, this harshness, that carries into future situations. It is this cynicism that has created the silence around a leader's mental health for far too long.

For a long time, I carried resentment.

Resentment was the poison I drank each day, feeling worn down by life and by work. It was in full force after Keane's death. We had achieved what we had dreamt for ourselves as sibling entrepreneurs, but he was no longer here. I was left with the aftermath of surviving: managing my mother's cancer and reconciling an abusive childhood, followed by a tragic adulthood.

How could your heart not go cold from that?

I know in working with tech founders and also corporate clients, many leaders of leaders have gone through their own reckoning. Of events that have pulled them down, from investors betraying them to co-founders leaving, on top of bankruptcies, lawsuits, and crises from their personal life. There have been plenty of mental health stories pledged by our #REALTALK Champions, prominent tech CEOs across North America, to showcase this pattern. I have sat with these leaders, who have been so open and so brave about sharing the human side of operating companies, while managing the craziness of life.

In trying to keep our head above water in such a fast-paced world, it is no wonder that many leaders of leaders numb out or avoid. In being with my own pain, the reality was that building #REALTALK was my cry for help. It was my solution to my own suffering.

I was tired of lying and pretending that things were okay. I had spent so many years hiding, avoiding, and numbing out with work and food, and now the dam broke. My vices were no longer a tenable solution, and I was faced with a stark reality: if I didn't heal my resentment and learn to be at peace with my past, I would carry this bitterness into every relationship and every company I build in the future.

In birthing #REALTALK into the world, I wanted to heal and connect with other founders and to have a community where I belonged. A community where I no longer needed to do things alone or to suffer in silence. My friend Jennifer Love, the former CEO of the national One More Woman movement, once told me, "Its real purpose is for you, and it has served its purpose."

She was referring to #REALTALK; I created this movement to heal *me*.

That conversation rocked me to my core.

As I sat with the implications of #REALTALK, it was true. In creating this movement, I held myself to the standard I always wanted. I finally had the courage to talk to my family about the hurt I experienced as a child and how it impacted me later in life. I cleaned up my personal and professional messes and became the leader of leaders, who could inspire and guide others through their darkness.

I was taking responsibility to another level: #REALTALK with You. I was cleaning up my past, all of the grudges I carried regarding others, so that I could be free.

I was stepping away from resentment and into forgiveness.

Many people start their career or business with a spark, only to lose that spark later on in life. To be hardened by betrayal and doubt, forgetting why we are here and who is supporting us. In the game of innovation, this resentment makes it hard for us to trust others and to lead teams effectively, especially with the level of authenticity and ease that we deeply crave. If we continue to lead from a heavy place, with all of our baggage from regrets to resentment, it will show up in our leadership and in our organization.

Not only is this an unsustainable way to lead, but it erodes the conditions for collaboration, co-creation, and initiative at a wider level. Like the #REALTALK Leadership model from Chapter Three, taking care of your mental and emotional well-being will unlock Calm (Thrive). Our financial and interpersonal needs are being met and we are sharing with others in a real way, giving us the space to delegate tasks and to breathe. With more capacity as a leader, it creates a foundation we can utilize in the future (#REALTALK with Us) in order to reconnect with our spark. The spark that fuels leaders to go beyond complacency and to start operating in extraordinary ways.

When I speak to large audiences around the world, I often get asked by the audience, "What motivates you to keep standing? What continues to fuel your work and the companies you build, despite what you've gone through in life?" It is in my honest belief, waking up each day, that life is tough. These times are tough, but each of us are here for a reason. And if you are going to engage in life, with everything that you've got, then it better be for the extraordinary life that you want. One that makes all of the pain, the sacrifice, and the wounds we bear in the workplace worth it.

As we wrap up #REALTALK with You, I challenge you to go beyond "just good enough" and to dream bigger. In a world that is struggling, we need leaders in action. We need leaders of leaders who are able to move humanity forward in ways that are productive, uplifting, and most of all, innovative.

It is time for us to come together.

THE RELATIONSHIP BETWEEN ANGER AND SADNESS

If resentment is the poison destroying leaders and their workplaces, what is the antidote? That word is forgiveness.

When we practice #REALTALK with You, we cast a light on our strengths and also our weaknesses. These weaknesses may be grievances, grudges, or hurt from past conversations, interactions, or situations. Over the course of years or even decades in building a career, it is not possible to be liked by everyone. You may have work relationships that turned sour, such as bosses taking credit for your work or co-founders who've bad-mouthed you behind your back.

The piling of these grievances starts out small, but without clearing those grievances, it continues to build until we have a landfill. A landfill that represents the mess we carry around as leaders.

Additionally, there is a tendency for people to complain, confront, or air out grievances to others and yet resist when the other side wants to speak. I have encountered this in my own life: when people reach out want-ing to talk, but the entire conversation is about them and they take up the oxygen in the room. They are scared to listen and to hear the impact they had on you, and the responsibility they held in that interaction.

In resisting the opportunity to understand and forgive others, resent-ment will build over time.

Internally, our team at #REALTALK has worked through resentment. My core team and I are survivors of mental health and trauma. When we hold spaces at organizations and events, the way we show up matters. If I am hosting a space on Diversity, Equity, and Inclusion (DEI), yet my own trauma around racism is unresolved, it can trigger the individuals I am trying to help.

This risk is especially true for the underrepresented and underprivi-leged, such as women and Black, Indigenous, and People of Color (BIPOC), who experience harm in many spaces. I often tell leaders who want to do DEI work that being a woman or a visible minority does *not* give you a free pass to facilitate these spaces. Being a woman does not mean that you have the skills or training to lead other women through this deep work. It is important that every leader trains and also processes their own relation-ship to emotionally charged topics. Otherwise, opening up those conversa-tions in your own community can do more harm than good, such as retriggering others.

In the world of healing, anger and sadness are two sides of the same coin and there is a level of care and intentionality that must be taken to move through those emotions.[1] **Anger** occurs after experiencing or witnessing a wrong, a desire to prevent or avoid harm. Anger is the expression of the word "no" and a way to exercise our boundaries with others. **Sadness** occurs after a significant loss, which allows us to acknowledge and process what is ending in our lives. Both emotions are necessary to function as a healthy human being, and it is healthy to process them on a regular basis rather than ignoring or numbing them out. Individuals will often reject or avoid a primary emotion (e.g. sadness) by expressing a secondary emotion (e.g. anger). For instance, individuals quick to anger struggle to access or express sadness and vice versa.

This pattern is especially found in men, where anger is accepted and shown in the media and in the workplace. We are bombarded with stories of men in movies (like the *Taken* series and the *John Wick* series), where their anger remains their only outlet to process the loss of loved ones. I can think of only a handful of movies where men were allowed to show their sadness *and* for that sadness to be accepted by those around them, rather than being judged and made emasculate. Sadness is mistaken as weakness much too often, as demonstrated beautifully and tragically in *The Iron Claw*, a movie about the Von Erich brothers from professional wrestling. It is this toxic culture that causes leaders of leaders, especially men, to close up their hearts and to lead alone.

There is a wounded heart that exists at the center of resentment. It is your inner child, who is lashing out because they are scared and even embarrassed to feel that way in the first place.

In resentment, we are trapped. No matter how much we achieve, including the right business and the right partner, we carry the past with us. Our past is incomplete, and we feel stuck, experiencing the same wrongs and asking ourselves, *Why do things feel so hard? Why do I feel so lonely? Why am I so unhappy?*

Resentment is like chains, dragging us back into the world we so badly want to escape.

Resentment, at the end of the day, represents something incomplete. There was something you needed to hear or something you needed to say, and it hasn't happened yet. You're keeping it all in. You're telling yourself things are okay when they are not.

The solution is to feel the anger and the sadness. By doing so, we create the opening for forgiveness, allowing us to move forward and be free.

WHAT IS FORGIVENESS?

Forgiveness is letting go of resentment and revenge so that we can create understanding and compassion for who or what hurt us. Forgiveness is a form of completion. In the world of high-performance coaching, **completion** means 100%: the act and choice of finishing something in its entirety, in order to move on with more peace and ease in your life.

Completion feels spacious like you can breathe, as your baggage stays *in the past.*

In life, everyone will get hurt at one point or another. We experience sabotage, lies, and trauma as flawed human beings interacting with other flawed human beings. Through forgiveness, we understand and accept what happened. Rather than resisting or avoiding the past, we are moving on regardless if other individuals (e.g. parents, colleagues) choose to do so.

In daily life, examples of forgiveness can be rare.

Anger and resentment have a level of righteousness, a temporary satisfaction that is comforting at first. In situations of danger like abusive relationships and racial violence, forgiveness can feel offensive or condescending to a survivor. How can I forgive that person who caused me physical, mental, emotional, or spiritual harm?

According to *Psychology Today*, the world's largest mental health magazine, the truth is that forgiveness is not:[2]

- Excusing the behavior or harm
- Forgetting the hurt or pain that occurred
- Saying it never happened
- Returning to what life was like before
- Sharing the blame in what happened

Forgiveness is a choice we make for ourselves each day because the way we are living is unworkable. The conversations we have with ourselves and others have become unworkable. It is dropping the Drama Triangle and the shoulds, which bring bitterness, disconnection, and misery, because you deserve better. Because you know the way you are showing up in your life and as a leader isn't it.

By acknowledging, processing, and coming to terms with our past, we can finally enjoy and be in the present. Instead of operating from grievances and hurt, we can be open to the moments, opportunities, and people in the present. We can stop self-sabotage and invite others to be part of the solution or the mission, instead of pushing them away.

The most exciting part? Completion, being 100%, has a transformational effect on our daily lives.

As humans, we rarely (if ever) complete things. Case in point, over 80% of New Year's Resolutions fail by February, such as losing weight or waking up earlier.[3] That is how much we don't complete things, dragging our past and our loops with us.

There is freedom and power that comes with completing things as leaders.

The oil company Syncrude Canada, which practices strict quality control, conducted research that demonstrated the difference between 99.9% and 100% completion. Here is what happens when we settle for 99.9% done:[4]

- This year, 2 million documents will be lost by the Internal Revenue Service (IRS).
- More than 880 000 credit cards will have incorrect cardholder information.
- This year, 114 500 mismatched pairs of shoes will be shipped.
- Every hour, 22 000 transactions will be deducted from the wrong bank accounts.
- Every minute, 1314 phone calls will be misplaced by telecommunication services.
- Twelve babies will be given to the wrong parents each day.

Forgiveness through completion is a way of cleaning up our past – no stone is left unturned. The more we practice this in every area of our lives, the more baggage we release and the more we can show up cleanly and powerfully as a leader of leaders. Imagine the leader who is able to show up for their organization, during the toughest of times, with a level of certainty, grace, and power toward a shared mission. Imagine the leader who leaves their baggage and their grievances at the door, and motivates others to do their best work, rather than lashing out and triggering their team?

Imagine how much further can you go as a leader of leaders without the baggage of your past.

HOW RECONCILIATION UNLOCKS PERFORMANCE

As you begin to heal yourself, your ability to lead will expand, shifting from #REALTALK with You (serving one to one) to #REALTALK with Us (serving many). My friend Theresa Laurico, one of Canada's most successful media entrepreneurs, once told me, "As you heal yourself, you heal the world."

When you are a leader, you have a disproportionate influence in every space you enter. As leaders, what we say and how we lead has a significant impact on our teams, our organization, and our industry. Your direct reports, your clients, and your partners look to your example to see what is acceptable or unacceptable behavior in the playing field, and they meet you there.

#REALTALK, North America's largest mental health movement for founders, started with one champion. One tech CEO stood up and said, "I will share my mental health story with you." His name was Sheetal Jaitly, CEO at TribalScale, and he demonstrated a new way of leading and sharing ourselves. He showed our peers, the other CEOs I wanted to recruit to this movement, that we could respond to the suffering of mental health with hope and courage, rather than with fear and resentment.

This potential to heal and to lead is not just for mental health but can occur in any other space, cause, or objective that matters to you. For instance, Woman of Color founders who have received venture capital represent less than 1% of all founders.[5] The tech industry has become known as "problematic," with scandals from the most successful companies like Airbnb (racism), Uber (sexual harassment), 500 Startups (sexual harassment), and Pinterest (gender discrimination). Their leaders or cultures have enabled or perpetuated these behaviors, causing an unsafe environment.

When your people are speaking out, how will leaders respond? Will you meet the occasion and use this grievance as an opportunity to heal and to do better?

For example, Airbnb's CEO Brian Chesky engaged in real talk, taking responsibility for the racist behavior on his platform.[6] He announced an anti-discrimination policy and admitted the breakdown in his leadership, where he was "slow to address these problems." He has partnered with online racial justice group Color of Change to combat systemic bias and discrimination in the future.

I speak of these issues because we live in an era of #MeToo and Black Lives Matter, where old systems are breaking down or are being challenged.

We are in a historic period in time, a reckoning and a reconciliation of past wrongs. We can allow the realness of these conversations to divide us, to feed into polarization and sensationalism, or we can come together to build a better future.

In my own world, I make the intentional choice each day to connect and collaborate with those who aren't like me. When I started as an entrepreneur 18 years ago, this wasn't a thing you had to say or declare. It was just the norm that you had friend circles and work circles where you didn't always agree with the people you were with, and that was okay.

In choosing the path of forgiveness and thus reconciliation, it unlocks a level of performance, collaboration, and creativity that has been missing in the world of work for so long. Despite being both a woman and a visible minority, I feel strongly that our world and our workplaces would be better if we weren't so angry. If we had the emotional stamina, resilience, and patience to be with a diversity of people, so that we could build bridges instead of walls.

This was the approach that my brother Keane and I took for so many years in our work. When we set out to tackle the global problem of financial inclusion, we wanted to first help customers that looked like us: Filipinos that came from poverty and lacked the financial education or means to engage in the digital economy. However, what was clear to us was that the solution wasn't going to be built by staying in our own circles. We had to reach out and work with people who had access to power and to circles that weren't our own. We partnered with a White co-founding family, another brother and sister duo, who came from generational wealth and knew the language of money like the back of their hand.

It was the combination of these diverse skillsets and networks that created high performance as an early team. It was this bridge that helped us punch far above our weight, in an industry and in a time where people didn't understand (and even feared) crypto and where the competition we were facing could outbuild and out-fund us at any moment.

As you consider these times, think about what forgiveness and releasing your baggage can do for you and your teams. How will you choose to lead at this moment in time?

INTERNAL EXERCISE: RELEASE CEREMONY

In the game of business and innovation, we are surrounded by colleagues and books that treat self-care as a doing, a literal to-do list. On my podcast show *#REALTALK with Cherry Rose Tan*, I teach self-care as a ritual and not a routine. A ritual takes away the pressure of doing something "wrong" by becoming an experience.

It becomes a gift that you want to give to yourself.

To build our ability to practice emotional self-care and forgiveness, we will start with a release ceremony. A **ceremony** is a special, time-bound experience or container where we can explore a sensitive topic (e.g. rage, grief) with care and intention. Once our ceremony is done, we close the container and return to our lives.

Instructions:

1. **Container:** Book a two-hour, uninterrupted block in your calendar where there is no work, no tech, and no family. Select a room where you can feel safe and relaxed, separate from your workspace. This ceremony is a solo experience for you to connect with you, with ample space for integration and self-care.
2. **Joy:** Bring objects that bring you joy and nourishment. These objects will vary from person to person. For example, I bring my photos of Keane and my leather-backed journals.
3. **Past:** Bring objects that continue to hold anger or sadness. It could be a photo of an ex that you continue to think about or a flyer of a previous business that failed.

4. **Ground:** Make yourself comfortable. You can sit on the floor, on a couch, or whatever brings you ease. Hold each object and think about your year. What was your life really like? How are you really doing at this moment?

5. **Feelings:** As you settle into this space, hold each object one by one. How does it make you feel? What is coming up for you?

6. **Release:** Take a piece of paper from your notebook. Write down all the things that you want to forgive. The *how* doesn't matter, merely your intention to let go. What have you been carrying that you're tired of carrying? What would you like to release?

7. **Integration:** Engage in a physical action that represents the release of those items. When I lead these exercises with founders, they come into the center of the room, declare the primary thing they are releasing, and then throw their paper in the fire.

Example: *I Release*

- My co-founder Douglas who had to step down
- The fact that I haven't spoken to my sister in a year
- Working 100 hours a week and losing my university friends
- Dating Mei and hurting her after the breakup
- "Not being good enough" to run this company

EXTERNAL EXERCISE: I FORGIVE

In this exercise, we move from forgiveness as a solo practice to engaging with others: #REALTALK with You. It means having conversations with the people in our lives where anger and sadness still exist.

A common mistake in emotional work is to stay in feeling but not take action.

When I rebranded our movement as #REALTALK, it moved me into action. I took stock of my own life and where I still carried resentment or hurt in my personal or professional relationships, especially with family. I had the tough but loving conversations with those individuals so that all of us could move on. I learned about the importance of not just acknowledging the hurt but of practicing forgiveness, in order to leave that heaviness behind.

In bringing forgiveness to real conversations with others, we can make new and harmonious choices.

Instructions:

1. **People:** Think of the individuals in your life whom you hold resentment for. They are people who have a disproportionate influence on your emotions, where you are upset by what they say and how they act. Having a conversation with them can feel like dread or frustration. Write down as many names as you can think of in the Person column.

2. **Feeling to Insight:** Finish one row (one individual) at a time. Write from left to right (five columns), in order to reach completion with that resentment, grievance, or grudge. What are you holding on to? What actions can you take to create healing in that relationship?

3. **Resolution:** Write, call, or meet that person to share these findings with them. Use your discretion in terms of whom to reach out to. In cases of active danger or harm, such as a toxic ex, you can adapt this exercise by addressing a letter to them instead. This letter stays with you, but it is important to release as much as you can for yourself. Allow the emotions through and give yourself the opportunity to heal.

Person	Feeling: I feel _____ when I think of you.	Wound: When you _____, it made me feel _____.	Impact: As a result, I continue to hold _____ around you.	Release: I choose to forgive you for _____.	Insight: By forgiving you, I understand _____.
Ryan (Co-Founder)	I feel betrayal when I think of you.	When you went behind my back, it made me feel unloved.	As a result, I continue to hold hostility around you.	I choose to forgive you for trying to replace me with another co-founder.	By forgiving you, I under- stand that you were scared of losing the company and that you did what you thought was best.
Annika (Ex-Wife)	I feel hurt when I think of you.	When you cheated, it made me feel less of a man.	As a result, I continue to hold hatred against you.	I choose to forgive you for getting drunk and having a one- night stand.	By forgiving you, I understand that our marriage wasn't working for years, especially in the bedroom.

THE SPACE FOR COMMUNITY

In practicing forgiveness, our ability to be real with others has a tangible impact in our workplaces and in our homes. Mental health is critical to every leader's longevity, and our ability to manage, process, and release the resentment and baggage we carry matters. It transforms whether we show up in spaces as our full selves, ready to be a catalyst for other leaders or if we are dragging others down because of our past. Leaders of leaders like yourself are in a unique position, where you are navigating difficult conversations with employees, vendors, partners, and more. This increased responsibility and influence on others is a double-edged sword: high pressure yet high opportunity.

Only those leaders of leaders who step up to the plate will experience the greatest of rewards: to mold themselves and their teams into something better. Even best.

As we step into the next part of this book (#REALTALK with Us), I congratulate you on the work you have done so far. In shifting your relationship to emotions from weakness to strength, we can lead our industry as the real and best versions of ourselves. We bring our emotional stamina and resilience into our daily work, so we can solve problems at the root and create the organizations that matter.

PART III

THE THIRD CONVERSATION

#REALTALK with Us

The third part, or Conversation, is having real conversations with your **community**, allowing your leadership to go beyond your immediate circles. This level of leadership holds the most business potential, where founders and leaders of leaders move from being operators of their organizations to being thought leaders in their industry. They become titans, gathering peers and mentors to support their cause. They are known not just for their expertise, product, or organization but for *who* they are.

This Conversation with community addresses the **Will (Actions)**. There is a noticeable shift in opportunities, events, and people that can support your organization. In our previous interviews with tech founders, momentum begins to build through meaningful wins and collaborations toward a particular goal. It could be an introduction to the right investor or a company that reaches out, wanting to work with you. Events are happening at the right place, at the right time, where founders and leaders of leaders shift from struggle and push to **creating abundance and pull**.

At #REALTALK, we have experienced sudden momentum with our work, after spending our initial year slogging it out. The more we put ourselves out there, the more people want to help. Results happen quicker, where your colleagues, supporters, and collaborators remember who you are and what you stand for. For instance, as our previous clients engage in conversations with their friends, family, and colleagues, #REALTALK becomes synonymous with workplace mental health and the tech industry. These people become our biggest champions and exponential progress can occur, even without our physical or live presence in every interaction.

CHAPTER NINE

IDENTITY

It was May 2020, a few months into COVID-19. So much change had occurred for our team at #REALTALK.

We went from an in-person model, speaking at conferences and organizations around the world, to online. In switching to digital, we released the podcast show *#REALTALK with Cherry Rose Tan*, hitting the Top 14 Business category on iTunes.

It was an incredible success for our team. We were releasing the Champion Stories through the podcast and our community had a way to connect with us. We were getting rave reviews for our work.

Suddenly, the existential questions came.

When I started #REALTALK, we built from this foundation of Champion Stories. They were stories collected over years from tech CEOs and investors, sharing the darkest moments of their career and how they got through them, capturing a moment in time. In recording those stories back then, I myself was raw from grief and processing the loss of my brother. By launching the podcast, there was a big emotional release.

I completed a promise I made when I started this movement: to break the stigma across the tech industry. The line was now drawn in the sand so that no founder would ever experience what my family went through. In the completion of this promise, I gave myself the permission to move on from this tragedy.

Now, there was space. For the first time, I was able to focus on something other than mental health and trauma. What came forth were questions about my identity and my heritage as a Filipino–Chinese Canadian woman.

Black Lives Matter was taking the global stage. Across our borders, millions of Americans were marching and protesting on the streets about systemic inequity, even in the midst of the pandemic. The conversation of trauma, one that I had been leading for years, was now acknowledging the layers of complexity that come with it, from gender to race.

Leaders were being called forward in their words and actions, not just in terms of their financials but their morals and what they stood for. It evoked something in me.

I spent so long *in the system*, excelling in an industry where senior leaders rarely (if ever) looked like me. I spent so long entering rooms of tech founders and investors being the only woman of color. I would stare at my library, a vast array of business books, and I realized that most of them were written by White men.

For the first time, I was able to explore questions about my lineage and my identity.

I was Chinese ethnically, but I couldn't speak the language. I spoke English all of my life, growing up and being educated here in Canada. I was Filipino by birth, but I didn't look like them. I was surrounded by anti-Asian messages in the media and a US government that named the pandemic the "China flu." I didn't fit into a box, and I was being approached by other founders, mostly women and visible minorities, who were struggling with similar issues around their identity and where they fit in.

They were feeling a conflict, a gap between the person they embodied in the tech industry and the person they really were. It was scary and exhausting to be surrounded by so much hostility and to wonder what was happening inside our workplaces and even our homes.

In a time of great uncertainty and also great anger, we needed to do something. We needed to come together to find a way forward, before it was too late.

FROM LEADER TO AUTHOR

As leaders of leaders, we can become extremely busy in the hustle and grind. We fill our personal and professional lives with "stuff," excuses for why our business, our marriage, or our health are failing.

In avoiding "real talk" with ourselves and others, we settle for mediocre or okay lives. We settle for keeping our head above water.

In stepping into #REALTALK with Us, we challenge this premise. We invite you to remember who you are and what you stand for as a leader of leaders. In my world of startups, we pride ourselves on creating the unicorn, the billion-dollar startup that will change the world. There is an insatiable drive, an unshakeable zeal to succeed and prove everyone else wrong. To challenge the status quo, break down systems, and usher in new ways of thinking.

This spark is what drew me to being a tech founder. This spark is what inspired the sibling-entrepreneur journey that Keane and I shared, using entrepreneurship to solve the world's problems. It is because of this spark that I get hired by corporations, associations, and universities around the globe who want to get a behind-the-scenes peak into the game of innovation at ground level.

As leaders of leaders, our spark can get eroded by the stresses and uncertainties we face on the journey. Looking at the #REALTALK

Leadership model, we settle for Complacency (good enough) where leadership is Calm (Thrive) and about managing people and culture. Thriving is still better than surviving, where our basic needs are met and our companies are growing, but it is missing the X factor, the *je ne sais quoi*. It is this X factor that pushes leaders to become extraordinary, to become best-in-class, and to build something that will stand the test of time.

You might be wondering to yourself, *What's wrong with just thriving? What if I am comfortable staying there? What if I'm okay with growing my business or my organization linearly?* The answer is: Thriving is a good place to be and a state we must be grateful for, given that many leaders are still trying to keep their heads above water.

However, it doesn't mean we have to stop there.

This last decade has challenged our definition of what it means to be great leader, a leader in these modern times. I think about this a lot in my own work as a keynote speaker, as an ecosystem builder, and as the Entrepreneur in Residence at Schulich, responsible for thousands of lives and hundreds of startups. Schulich Startups are doing revolutionary things in over 27 different verticals, pushing the envelope on industries old and new (like real estate, finance, and more) and also on exponential technologies like artificial intelligence.

What have I learned about leadership, that continues to fire the spark in me until this day?

As someone who was there in the earliest days and conversations around crypto, then around AI, my belief is that the greatest and most prolific organizations are yet to come. In the face of some of the largest challenges this world has faced, we are at another flashpoint where there is immense opportunity. That for the bravest and most willing of us, the leaders of leaders who embody real talk into their everyday fabric of who they are, what will emerge from this crucible is a type of leader who will pave the way for us and future generations.

In the startup industry, they understand this. That the top startups, the eventual market leaders of the industry, are run by a special type of leader with this mix. We call them **founders** for a reason. The word "founder" itself (like in the old days when sailors found treasure and entire regions of the planet) has the word *found* in it, which implies discovery, newness, and potential.

Beyond Complacency, leadership can become a form of Creation (Author) and about building a shared future. Returning to the truest definition of the founder, we can become the literal authors of our industry. #REALTALK is no longer about Me or You, but about *Us*.

A collective Us, at the level of community, industry, or planet, where the way we speak and lead transforms the game as we know it. In scaling our leadership to hundreds or even millions of people, our leadership is made exponential. The mission or possibility becomes reality, and the best thing is: we aren't doing this alone. We are surrounded by capable leaders who we have cultivated over time because of how we show up in the workplace. It is these future leaders that will strengthen our stand and our impact, should we choose this multiyear journey of innovation and business.

Given the very grave and systemic problems our world is facing, the boldness and expansion of leadership matters. It is the leadership the planet needs at this time. It is the leadership that paves for titans of industry.

THE UNRAVELING

To lead from Creation (Author), we must understand the life cycle of a business.

One of my favorite psychometric tools is Wealth Dynamics, the world's leading profiling tool for entrepreneurs. Its creator, Roger Hamilton, studied over 250 000 entrepreneurs around the world, and he discovered the cycle of entrepreneurship mirrors that of nature.[1] The four seasons from spring to winter mirror the cycle of life (and death), as plants grow and then die, only for new ones to birth in their place.

For a tech leader like myself, these plants are our startups.

In VC and startups, we use terminology influenced by nature, such as early investment rounds being named Pre-Seed or Seed. This lifestyle matters because the creation of ideas, products, or services occurs after death, when the old clear out. We need physical, mental, and emotional space to create the next company or embark on the next relationship. Terms like exit and post-exit for founders are intentional to indicate these stages.

Why are we not this way with ourselves and our leadership?

In letting go of the past, as done through forgiveness, we can breathe. We have the space to shift from doing (the day-to-day operations of the company) to being (an understanding of *who* we are as leaders). It is an **unraveling**: reevaluating and unlearning ourselves so that we understand what is true (ours) and what is other (stories, identities, and paradigms that were put onto us and no longer serve us).

This unraveling is not isolated to the individual. The planet is going through it too.

As humanity embarks on real talk together, our systems are being challenged. Communities are speaking out about sexism, racism, and mental health. Intergenerational trauma has become a prominent topic in the #REALTALK community, as founders grapple with the effects of inherited systems. We have made significant strides in including leaders of all walks of life into these conversations, including White men, who can be allies and in some cases are survivors themselves through experiences like mental illness, poverty, and addiction.

The consequences of intergenerational trauma have created the rise of psychedelic medicine, where MDMA and psilocybin are being used to treat post-traumatic stress disorder (PTSD), a disease that has seen little progress through traditional therapy. This work is so important that the US Food and Drug Administration (FDA) has granted "breakthrough therapy" status to psilocybin, accelerating the process of drug development and review.[2]

Working on your trauma has become a commonplace topic in my own circles, surrounded by other CEOs who are getting in their own way as leaders (often through self-sabotage). They are realizing that it is not just what they do that matters but *who* they are when they do it. If we know who we are and we hold an incredible context for our lives, both personally and professionally, it drives the kind of collaboration and momentum that creates leaders and opportunities all around us.

In healing my own trauma, I accepted my physical, cultural, and racial identity. In forgiving my family, I learned about the physical and financial hardships my ancestors experienced in moving to and building a life in the Philippines. I learned about the corruption and the violence they saw on a daily basis, growing up in a politically unstable country. I learned about how hard my parents had to work to provide a life for myself and Keane in Canada, in order to access the opportunities they never had.

In understanding this backdrop, I saw how my own identity as a leader had been tied to the immigrant story of "working very hard" and in patterns of workaholism that Keane and I demonstrated in our twenties. I had been a lone wolf for so long, with a chip on my shoulder and something to prove. The founder that worked 80- to 100-hour weeks, achieving the accolades and success, but never feeling happy because I was working myself to the bone and not delegating or trusting others. I kept holding and defending a story that it was solely I, Cherry Rose Tan, that could complete this task or handle this client.

Being a lone wolf and a martyr was toxic and unsustainable in the long run. It was the thing holding me back from my greatness as a leader and as an organization.

When we start making the space to explore *who* we are as leaders, we begin to unlock a new level of performance and leadership. One that can make an exponential difference at the level of community and industry, the kind necessary for these difficult times.

WHY IDENTITY MATTERS

To scale real talk, we must understand the role of identity. Every layer of communication, verbal and nonverbal, is affected by our **identity.** The way we listen and interpret our world is dependent on our demographics and psychographics, shaped by the experiences we have lived.

Demographics are the distinct characteristics of a population used to study groups and entire communities. Examples of demographics, which are used in censuses and marketing, include age, race, ethnicity, gender, marital status, income, education, and employment. When we think about the politically or emotionally charged conversations happening in the global sphere, it is often occurring at the level of demographics: who we deem as one of us (our in-group) and who does not belong (the out-group). As you can imagine, the members of the in-groups and the out-groups will change drastically depending on your own identity as a leader of leaders.

On the other hand, **psychographics** are the cognitive characteristics of a population, such as activities, interests, and opinions. Within a defined demographic, there are differences in emotional triggers, life-style choices, personal goals, and more. Psychographics give us an intimate look into the world of an individual, and lean startup tools like Value Proposition Canvas are used in the earliest stages of building a product or service because every company must provide value to their customers to survive. We can only know how to create and unlock value when we understand the pain points of that customer and what they desire.

A subset within psychographics, it is important for us as leaders to know our **core values:** our fundamental beliefs that guide our decisions and actions on a daily basis. Our core values are at the root of our leadership and affect what priorities we hold, plus what we need as leaders to feel supported and fulfilled. In my work coaching CEOs and executives, I ask them their core values in the first call and many of them can't answer this. When I dig deeper, these leaders are unable to tell me why they have made past decisions or commitments with clarity because they don't know who they are. They don't have a set of values with which to discern and create in the world.

Thus, in combining demographics (the *who*) with psychographics (the *why*), we can connect with people from all walks of life (stakeholders in both our personal and professional lives) in a compelling and authentic way. As a leader of leaders, demographics and psychographics inform our own identity and that of others, so that we can build bridges and communicate relevant messages to rally people toward a shared cause or objective, such as innovation.

As leaders of leaders, much of our influence and success is dependent on our relationships. We spend years networking with the right investors, advisors, partners, and clients in order to gain as many allies as possible. We learn what to share and how to share, to paint an exciting and powerful image of our companies to the media and our industry.

Mastering communication, especially its nuance, is critical for leading in these times. Communicating in compelling ways may also mean the difference between a team or an organization that rallies alongside the new, multi-year strategy you just proposed, and an organization of employees that fights you tooth-and-nail with every change and implementation because you don't have their buy-in. I serve on the Board of Directors for two national charities in healthcare, where the challenges are complex and have serious implications at the community level, and our communication matters.

HOW IDENTITY AFFECTS COMMUNICATION

The main tenet throughout this book is that **real talk is a necessary condition of leadership.** Being able to master and scale tough conversations creates the kind of unshakeable leadership that innovation desires. It is also the inspiration behind the title of this book *Still Standing*: acknowledging that leaders need a level of emotional and business resilience to win the game of innovation, which can be cultivated through intentional practice.

When we speak of identity, we do so because all conversations are affected by the identities of the person speaking and the person listening. Every piece of communication has two layers: content and context. **Content** is the information we share with our intended audience, like the topics covered in media articles and blog posts. **Context**, on the other hand, is the positioning of the content, which provides its meaning and value to the audience. Two individuals can see the same political commercial (Content) but have different interpretations of what happened (Context).

As the saying goes, "Context, not content, is king."

Identity is context, neither good nor bad, but it is always there. As humans, identity can never disappear, but we can become aware of it.

During my #REALTALK days, identity was an important factor for us to navigate by honoring the experiences these founders lived through, plus the context they held around mental health and self-care. Many founders (and even investors) would approach us privately to share their mental health stories because "they had nowhere else to go." In building a sense of trust with them, we were able to build strong communities of founders for tactical and business reasons too. After all, once you have a circle of people that you can share anything with, how does that affect your ability to share your greatest challenges head-on? To ask for help and support in the most powerful of ways?

Embodying real talk is not just for our overall well-being; it creates a level of sharing that maximizes your potential as a leader of leaders. Identity also plays a huge role in the safety and trust that is necessary in order for real talk to occur. Depending on the identity one holds (e.g. woman of color), it shifts the barriers and risks associated with sharing openly and bravely in the workplace and at home.

For instance, having an extra layer of safety based on your gender, race, or socioeconomic status can go a long way as to whether or not you make that bold ask of that client or investor. This consideration has only amplified in the last few years, where this uneven playing field has widened since the pandemic. In the first nine months of COVID-19, *USA Today* reported that "America's 614 billionaires grew their net worth by a collective $931 billion."[3] Total billionaire wealth on the planet surged to a record high of $10.2 trillion, from $8 trillion at the start of the pandemic. While the lower class struggled, the wealthy got wealthier.

These systemic gaps have trickle-down effects on our workplaces and the people we work with too. In a May 2024 article by *The Hub*, they reported the record-low fertility rates emerging in Canada and its relationship to financial stability. In the first five years of parenthood, the average decrease in earnings is 40% for Canadian women and 0.5% for men.[4] Researchers found that this impact on earnings is the leading cause in Canadian women's decision not to have children, where our national fertility rate is a record-low of 1.33.

When we think about the multiple pressures each of us are facing, how does it affect our workplace and what our employees need? What do our future leaders need in order to feel confident and prepared to meet the challenges of today?

The gaps are increasing and we are heading toward a point of no return, where we have to act before it is too late.

Real talk and participating in our social, financial, and cultural systems is not an equal opportunity yet. However, we can create structures to manage risk and reduce harm so that #REALTALK with Us becomes possible. This approach, which we call intersectionality, has been our secret sauce for creating real conversations among C-Suite leaders.

WHAT IS INTERSECTIONALITY?

In 1991, the term *intersectionality* was cited in law professor Kimberlé Crenshaw's article called *Mapping the Margins*. She noticed that people who are "both women and people of color" face disproportionate risk and exclusion by "discourses that are shaped to respond to one [identity] or the other."[5]

According to the *Oxford English Dictionary*, **intersectionality** is the "interconnected nature of social categorizations such as race, class, and gender, regarded as creating overlapping and interdependent systems of discrimination or disadvantage."

What does this mean in real life?

When an individual is part of two or more categorizations, where each category faces discrimination, the risk for that individual increases. For instance, White women founders do not experience the same barriers as Black women founders. The latter experience both sexism *and* racism, having to navigate both simultaneously. At the same time, intersectionality is not about dismissing or marginalizing the experiences of others, since mental health and trauma affect people from all walks of life. It merely gives us deeper lenses into understanding the circumstances that our people are experiencing and how we can connect, lead, and motivate them more effectively.

Feminist leaders Linda E. Carty and Chandra Talpade Mohanty note that for White women, "her whiteness will always protect and insulate her from racism." In comparing two individuals, Carty and Mohanty emphasize that they "do not experience the same levels of discrimination, even when they are working within the same structures."

As a Filipino-Chinese Canadian from Manila, Philippines, my ancestors are survivors of war and poverty. The Philippines was colonized by Spain in the 1500s, and many of our Indigenous people, along with our languages and cultures, were displaced. It caused instability in the region (e.g. physical, financial), which continues until this day, due to a heavy military presence by local entities and other countries. There have been several coup d'états over the decades, as leaders are overthrown and assassinations occur.

There is a loss of identity, heritage, and pride in the Filipino culture, where Filipinos are seen as "less than" by other Asians due to colourism, where lighter-skinned Asians are "more respected." Filipinos also face discrimination from non-Asian cultures, who associate Filipinos as nannies, housekeepers, and nurses.

It is this understanding of intersectionality that informs the safety, intimacy, and depth of what we do at #REALTALK. As one of the only women of color in the spaces I enter, I have experienced intersectionality and its increased risk.

For example, March 2021 brought forth the Atlanta shootings, where eight people died, six of whom were Asian women.[6] There was a 600–700% increase in violence against Asian Canadians in the year following COVID-19 and a 1900% increase in violence against Asian Americans in New York.[7] These incidents targeted Asian women, and physically taller or larger men were the instigators. I experienced two racial incidents during the same time period, along with two Asian women founders in my Toronto circle.

In earlier chapters, we talked about the difference between danger (bodily harm) and fear (psychological threat). In engaging in real talk and bringing it forward as leaders, we must understand that the costs of participation are not equal. There will be members of our community who will experience both danger and fear, while others will only experience fear. For us to come together and have real talk, we must be intentional in our leadership.

Too often in my work with clients, I am hired by the CEOs of these organizations (many of them million-dollar or billion-dollar corporations) because they are facing change resistance. My most popular keynote is called *Possibility Executed™: Determining the Future of Your Organization in an Age of Uncertainty*, where I talk about the mindset, heartset, and skillset needed to build the future without burning out. These CEOs hire me because they are about to (or have) declared a new strategy, often innovation-focused in nature, only to find out that their people are upset.

Or even worse, pissed off because they are tired and feel overworked as it is, unable or unwilling to add another thing to their plates. For them, they see additional responsibilities as tone-deaf by their bosses and CEOs.

Having intersectionality allows us to engage with stakeholders of all walks of life, ones that look like us and ones that don't, so we can avoid the scenario I just mentioned. Wouldn't your job be so much easier if you could get stakeholders on your side? If you could get your employees to say yes and to work with one another on a shared mission or strategy?

That is the power of #REALTALK with Us, bringing these tough conversations to a level of scale where we can create future-proof, resilient organizations against the storms of innovation.

CREATING TRAUMA-INFORMED SPACES

We speak about intersectionality at #REALTALK because psychological safety and mental health are never separate from identity. This work ties back to workplace mental health because we are facing a worldwide epidemic when it comes to burnout and other mental health–related conditions at work, such as depression and anxiety. This trend has only worsened in light of the pandemic, the recession, and also the advent of AI, where the pressures to change and adapt are faster than ever.

The fact is that every organization will have a diversity of people working there, and your most underrepresented team members will experience more stress, harm, and barriers when it comes to mental health treatments or supports. Mental Health America notes that Black, Indigenous, and People of Color (BIPOC) experience the **treatment gap**: "BIPOC populations are more vulnerable to mental health issues than non-BIPOC populations and use mental health services less often."[8] For instance:

- Black Americans are 20% more likely to experience depression, ADHD, and PTSD.
- Black and Latino Americans use mental health services half as often as White Americans.
- Asian Americans use mental health services a third as often as White Americans.

The Centre for Addiction and Mental Health (CAMH), Canada's largest mental health hospital, is addressing the bias in another way. In March 2020, CAMH launched womenmind, a philanthropic community that is tackling gender issues in mental health. They note that "treatments used today have been disproportionately tested on men and not equitably studied in women."[9] In the world of VC and startups, we are seeing the rise of a vertical known as **femtech:** software and services addressing problems related to women's health, which represented untapped billion-dollar opportunities.

In scaling real talk to our communities, intersectionality can be a strength rather than a curse. It challenges us to design and enter spaces in more thoughtful ways. When my team works with organizations, we manage these considerations by embodying two practices:

1. **Harm Reduction:** a set of practices to reduce the negative physical, mental, or social consequences of participation.
2. **Risk Mitigation:** a set of methods and strategies to reduce the anticipated and/or potential risks of that situation.

The difference between harm reduction and risk mitigation is that the former is based on equitable practices, with an understanding that certain individuals may be disproportionately impacted by preexisting trauma or systemic barriers in opportunities or spaces. This conversation is tied into the current conversation of culturally informed practices that are responsive to the needs of business leaders, their team members, and even your customers as you expand as a company. On the other hand, risk mitigation is more encompassing, focusing less on the present harm that is already in the system and more on the future threat that may or may not come. The intention is that if we mitigate these factors ahead of time, we can prevent harm from occurring in the first place.

The two in combination (backward thinking and forward thinking) create trauma-informed spaces that are powerful containers for real talk. These spaces go from being intimidating or stressful environments that people avoid to welcoming and collaborative environments that address problems, clear grievances, and create solutions as a collective. This version of real talk creates incredible levels of accessibility and safety that empower your people to become leaders, while increasing your capacity to pursue new responsibilities or opportunities.

The business potential is endless, and by knowing the identity and experiences that each individual brings, we can lead more skillfully and gracefully as leaders.

INTERNAL EXERCISE: THE STORIES WE CARRY

To hold space for others, we need to understand our identity and the experiences, biases, and trauma that come with it. What are the stories that we have inherited? How has our biological, cultural, and social lineage shaped the way we live and lead?

Instructions:

1. **Generations:** Take a large piece of paper. Draw five generations of your family tree, starting with your name at the bottom and moving upward. Write down as many names as possible from your parental lineages, drawing lines to show relationships.

2. **Experiences:** Once the names are complete, start from your name again and move upward. For each individual, write down the mental illness, trauma, or adverse event they have experienced. Write as keywords, keeping it short and brief (e.g. depression, domestic violence).

3. **Patterns:** Look at the keywords you have written. If a keyword appears more than once, take a colored highlighter and highlight all occurrences of that pattern. Do the same for any keywords that repeat, selecting a new color each time.

4. **Observations:** Using the following questions, take stock of your family tree:

   - What do you notice? What are you realizing?
   - Out of all the experiences, which ones stand out? Is there a pattern?
   - Are there one or more experiences (e.g. depression) that appear elsewhere on the tree? What are you learning about your family?
   - Are there one or more experience(s) that appear in just your generation? If so, can you recall how it/they started?

Experience	Years	Generations	Triggers
Poverty	8	2	Foster homes
Depression	5	2	Domestic violence
Anxiety	5	1	Financial instability
Grief	3	2	Grandfather's passing

EXTERNAL EXERCISE: WHAT THEY SAY

A huge part of understanding our identity is deconstructing the past and our current stories from society, which has shaped that identity. For example, how does the media talk about Asian women? What did I hear about women and tech careers when I was growing up in school?

Instructions:

1. **Demographic and Identity:** Follow the format below. For each variable under Demographic, write down how it represents your identity.
2. **Dialog:** Complete the table, row by row. What are people saying about this particular demographic in the media, in our schools, and in our communities?
3. **Impact:** Sit with yourself and the implications of this dialog. How has listening to these events, stories, and opinions affected you growing up? How does it affect you now as an adult and as a leader of leaders?
4. **Deconstruction:** Given everything you wrote, what are the two demographic identities which could benefit the most from healing? What is one action you will take for each in order to accept and honor your identity?

Demographic	Identity	Dialog: What do people say about this demographic?	Impact: How did it affect you growing up? Now?
Age	Gen Z	We just need to "work harder" to succeed. Don't value or understand commitment.	My family didn't understand how tough it was for me growing up. Thought I wasn't trying hard enough.
Race	Chinese	"Model minority" → people think we don't need help. Lots of hostility against Chinese people during COVID-19.	Conflicted and distant from my culture. Confused by the negative messages in Western media.
Gender	Female	Common to experience microaggressions and/or inappropriate situations. "Women are bad at math."	My teachers told me that it was okay if I gave up. Felt very alone → the only woman in most rooms.

MOVING TOWARD THE GREATER GOOD

Being with our identity, which includes our experiences and its layers, is not easy. In looking at ourselves in the mirror, we begin to understand *who* we are as leaders and as people. By acknowledging the social and cultural dynamics in our lives and in the workplace, we can begin to evaluate and create better systems for all stakeholders, both internal and external.

Leaders like us have the opportunity to lead on a much grander scale, acknowledging and integrating our identity as we do so. Instead of being the leader that polarizes and diminishes others, we can be the catalyst: the catalyst for change, the catalyst for innovation as each organization seeks to become future-proof, relevant, and valuable this decade.

We can become the reliable and safe presence that opens up conversation and collaboration with people that are like us *and* people that aren't like us at all. We become the person that builds bridges and activates opportunities because of our ability to connect and communicate. In the next chapter, we learn to reclaim our power and our communities using our advantages and disadvantages for the better good.

CHAPTER TEN

RECLAMATION

It was July 2021 and for the first time in a long time, I was hopeful.

It had been a year and a half since the pandemic, and myself and my team found our bearings. The #REALTALK movement was near and dear to our hearts, to every stakeholder from my team to our champions and our sponsors. However, COVID-19 had impacted us deeply and the future of our organization.

In watching fellow colleagues, we saw how other movement-based companies had closed down. So many of these movements, including #REALTALK, relied on revenue streams like event tickets and in-person brand activations in order to keep going, and now the well was dry. What do you do in a situation where your people depend on you? What do you do when you need to pivot quickly and swiftly with little resources in play?

I was also going through an existential crisis of my own. One of my most important and sacred traditions as an entrepreneur is to select a theme for each decade. Keane and I started this practice together when we were teens, choosing a theme or problem that we would commit to solving for an entire decade. A problem that we felt was worth solving so that if we aimed for the moon and landed on the stars, the journey itself (and who we would become as leaders) would be worth it.

This decade, I was beginning to realize that my world was shifting. In leading the #REALTALK movement the last three years, I began to notice a small and growing pattern. Even though we had worked with tens of thousands of leaders at this point, we began to hit a wall as a collective. Our founders would come to our events and have a transformative experience. A feeling that they were no longer alone and that they had the mindset, heartset, and skillset to lead themselves and their teams.

However, what these founders continued to struggle with was how to integrate back into the broader ecosystem. Time and time again, our founders would tell us that they understood the importance of their mental and physical health and they wanted to see these practices brought into their organizations. But when they brought up real talk or mental health to other stakeholders, like their board directors or their investors, it was often met with misunderstanding and even resistance. There wasn't a shared language on the planet around mental health back then, and these founders were having a hard time gathering the necessary buy-in to make these changes and their well-being long-lasting.

With this realization, it set me on a different journey.

I needed to make a fundamental shift in my work. It wasn't enough to operate at the level of founders; we needed to engage with *all* stakeholders in our ecosystem, especially those with the most power in my industry. I wanted to dedicate the next decade of my life to solving **generational wealth**, looking at systems of power and money and seeing how we could level the playing field. How we could remove the barriers preventing tech founders (and now leaders of leaders around the world) from accessing the resources, mentorship, and money they need to innovate *and* to thrive while doing so.

It was with this insight that I began to have conversations discreetly and behind closed doors, about my desire to enter into the venture capital space. I wanted to be on the other side of the table, in rooms of power, and to be able to shape the policy and the practices that affected (and even dis-empowered) so many founders in their own companies. I would be able to continue the journey I started at #REALTALK by being the kind of investor who could advocate for workplace mental health.

To make this leap would require not just the determination I knew I had in life, but a different approach. I needed a comprehensive strategy, one that was tactical and thorough. Where could I begin?

THE COLLECTIVE ILLUSION

The world is experiencing a rude awakening. In the business world, the COVID-19 pandemic has been labeled a **black swan**: a sudden and unpredict-able event that causes tremendous change, defying previous rules or patterns.

A black swan cannot be prepared for.

COVID-19 is such an event. Entire industries like real estate, hospital-ity, and retail were going out of business in record numbers. Even after the travel restrictions disappeared, industries like commercial real estate have not recovered to their pre-pandemic numbers. When we pay attention to the global dialog on innovation and uncertainty, COVID-19 is not just a black swan; this entire decade is.

Like waking up from the Matrix, people are becoming present to the collective illusion: that many of our responsibilities, roles, and expectations are man-made, meaning they can be challenged and even redefined. We inflict these stories on ourselves or even each other. According to Dr. Erin Cech, Associate Professor of Sociology at the University of Michigan, COVID-19 has been a "destabilizing moment" where people are question-ing what they value in their lives.[1]

We were once hamsters on a wheel, accepting the circumstances given to us. With this interruption by COVID-19, we saw things anew.

By interrupting long-standing patterns, like commuting to a nine-to-five job, this pause created space for people to think. *Forbes* called the pandemic "The Great Pause," stating, "The pandemic has forced people to stop and think about what they really want to do. That signals massive changes in government, commerce, and society."[2]

In Chapter Two, we referred to this moment in history as a Brave New World. In bracing ourselves for this new world, there are two workplace trends that have emerged from this awakening:

Quiet Quitting

The first trend that has emerged is **quiet quitting**, where employees are meeting the minimum requirements in their 9-5 job, but not going beyond it. A form of counterculture, employees are tired and skeptical of the promises that the workplace or society has promised them. As a professor to students aged 22–35, I see this skepticism in my day-to-day interactions, where the prices for basic living have skyrocketed in comparison to the increases in salaries. As a result, employees are fighting back against unhealthy workplace practices like working their employees extremely long (and often underpaid) hours.

Additionally, these employees are challenging the boundaries of multiple stakeholders, such as their bosses, their colleagues, and their clients. Boundaries are a way to reclaim your power and your voice, as you advocate for what you need and the change you want to see.

The newer generations, particularly Gen Z, have become outspoken about the importance of being treated well in the workplace too. They expect and demand their bosses to treat their employees as human beings, not machines. For instance, multinational insurance company Cigna conducted their Global Well-Being Survey in 2022 and found that 91% of Gen Zs are stressed, 98% said they are burned out, and 34% cited uncertainty about the future as their key stressor.[3] In that same study, they found that

48% of Gen Z say that work feels "transactional" without the ability to bond with colleagues. For them, feeling connected to and valued by their workplace matters.

These boundaries are so important to the employees of today that for many, they are considered non-negotiable. Gympass did a study in 2023 reporting that 78% of Gen Z employees would leave a company that doesn't focus on emotional well-being, and that well-being at work is equally important to salary.[4]

Quiet quitters are not a small or fringe group either – they are becoming more mainstream. In 2022, Gallup found that quiet quitters make up at least 50% of the US workforce, which is a conservative estimation by their standards.[5] Additionally, the ratio between engaged employees (32%) and actively disengaged employees (18%) is the lowest in a decade, sitting at a ratio of 1.8:1.

The effects of quiet quitting and even job resignations are not solely in the "lower ranks," but affect leaders of leaders as well. Managers are the level of the organization that have experienced the greatest drop in engagement on the job. All stakeholders are impacted negatively when leaders are unable to balance the need for innovation and high performance with the need for mental health and sustainable workplaces. Thus, the game of innovation is no longer about pursuing success at all costs, but doing it in a way that aligns all stakeholders and satisfies their needs.

Change Rage

The second trend emerging from the ashes of the collective illusion is change rage. In having to face or address the pressures of innovation, workplaces and their people are cracking under pressure. This trend will continue to grow as the pace of innovation outpaces the ability of leaders to cope with that change. In previous years, you might have heard of the term **change fatigue**, where leaders and their employees have become burnt out because of the massive amounts of change and information they are dealing with each day. A 2022 study of 1000 US-based employees found that 71% are overwhelmed by the amount of change that has happened at their job and that 54% of change-fatigued employees are considering looking for a new job.[6]

To understand this growing problem, we need to understand how exponential technologies like AI have escalated these pressures. In 2023, the American Psychological Association (APA) conducted their first ever AI-related study, looking at the effects of AI on workplace mental health.[7] APA found that worrying about AI is associated with stress and burnout, with 64% of employees feeling tense or stressed during the workday, compared with 38% who did not worry about AI. These findings were driven by fears that employees will lose some or all of their jobs in the future, which is a plausible scenario depending on their industry.

A few months ago, I was sitting with a prominent C-Suite executive who was in charge of a $500 million budget and whose decisions affected millions of people. Every decision was high-stakes for their organization, where an excellent decision could lift an entire community, while a bad decision could doom it.

In talking to this executive about their organization's needs, we discussed the trends of burnout in the workplace. Change fatigue currently persists across so many industries, and this executive told me that "change fatigue" was too kind of a term to explain how employees feel nowadays. Some organizations, especially those that lack tough and honest conversations, are feeling **change rage.** That not only are employees exhausted and overworked at managing the responsibilities they were initially hired for, but introducing new technologies or innovation can elicit feelings of anger, frustration, and even resentment. A feeling that the "people at the top" are out-of-touch, unable to understand that employees are overwhelmed and not "wanting more onto their plate."

Given these emotionally charged dynamics, since all human beings were not built to handle this level of change, what can we do differently? How do we show up as leaders for ourselves, our teams, and our organizations, while addressing the very real realities and stressors of our people? How do we create the healthy and high-performing cultures to meet these challenges, rather than fold beneath them?

FROM ANGER TO RECLAMATION

In the world right now, there is an underlying anger (and even rage) in many areas of life. As people wake up from the collective illusion in their personal and professional lives, the first emotion that often comes through will be anger. In Chapter Eight, we talked about the importance of anger as an emotion and how it relates to sadness. Anger is a useful emotion to signal when our boundaries have been violated or when we have operated below our standards, so that we can restore them. Anger is also a key foundation in restoring our voice and our power, a rallying call or **reclamation** to do better and to hold the line.

In the world of media, we are seeing this phenomenon everywhere. Since the pandemic, we have seen individuals and entire communities reclaim their power in the public sphere:

Financial Inclusion

During COVID-19, a popular Reddit forum called r/wallstreetbets made history by coordinating retail investors against Wall Street.[8] A retail investor is a nonprofessional investor who purchases assets like stocks and securities through a third party (e.g. brokerage firm). They tend to be "regular" citizens looking to build their wealth, such as a teacher who invests their savings for retirement. Wall Street is made up of institutional investors, companies, or organizations that invest large amounts of money on behalf of their clients, such as hedge funds.

In January 2021, retail investors caused GameStop stock prices to rise significantly, a company that was predicted to go bankrupt. By betting against the position of hedge funds, these institutional investors lost billions of dollars and many have closed down. Citizens are aggregating their power to choose, questioning existing platforms like Nasdaq and Robinhood, which face claims of interfering or blocking citizens from trading. It caused the US Securities and Exchange Commission (SEC) to start an investigation of Robinhood, which prevented users from buying shares in GameStop and seven others.[9]

Capturing the zeitgeist of the times, users of r/wallstreetbets celebrated this historic moment with a five-second ad during Super Bowl LV, stating: "Powerful things happen when people rally around something they really care about."

Food Security

Another topic that has become a rallying point for the masses is the afford-ability and security of food. In Canada, one of the most popular subreddits of 2024 is r/loblawsisoutofcontrol. Loblaw Companies is a billion-dollar corporation and the largest Canadian food retailer, owning supermarkets like Loblaws, No Frills, T &T Supermarket, and Shoppers Drug Mart. Citizens are currently boycotting Loblaws and its other affiliated compa-nies because Canadians are struggling to make ends meet. The ability to afford basic necessities like food, especially after working at least one full-time job, has been a major focus on the Canadian political sphere. In addi-tion to food security, the public has been re-evaluating the policies around immigration and how it has affected both the job market and the rental prices for Canadians who already live here.

In some cases, this anger has boiled into a rage, where Global News reported that Steal from Loblaws posters have appeared across Toronto.[10] Debates have appeared on the national sphere as to what is the right way to protest, and how we can create systemwide change in a way that sets a positive example for future generations. With frustrations at a boiling point and the major political parties avoiding the topic, citizens continue to self-organize without a clear leader of leaders to guide them.

Housing Affordability

The hot button issue of housing and rental affordability has also entered the main sphere, bringing heated discussions between tenants and landlords. Many Canadians believe that buying a home is out of reach in comparison to when their parents were their age, with 71% of Gen Z (ages 18–24), 69% of younger Millennials (ages 25–34), and 65% of older Millennials (ages 35–44) holding these views.[11] It has caused forums like r/canadahousing to emerge in its wake, where this topic draws frustration and also rage.

Housing affordability has reached a boiling point that Prime Minster Justin Trudeau announced Canada's Housing Plan, a component to be included in the upcoming Budget 2024. Its goal is to unlock 3.87 million new homes by 2031 through the provision of loans, using rental payment history to improve credit scores, and extending mortgage amortizations for first-time buyers.[12] It has also caused the emergence of companies that are looking to solve these problems such as Openroom, which is creating transparency in the rental ecosystem by allowing tenants and landlords to upload and view court orders of bad players in the ecosystem. Launched in January 2023 by Weiting Bollu, a Schulich BBA graduate who had a distressing experience as a landlord while pregnant, CBC News reported that her database has hosted almost 2 million searches in the last 12 months, all from organic traffic.[13]

In seeing these examples and in waking up from the collective illusion, the Us in #REALTALK is angry. In losing businesses, relationships, and more, there is a universal grief, followed by anger. It is clear that the status quo is unbearable for many and that the frustration and rage have affected people in the workplace, with trends like quiet quitting and change rage in order to exercise their boundaries and their rights.

In re-evaluating the status quo, we ask ourselves as leaders of leaders: How can our workplaces and our organizations be different? How can we create a world that works for more people?

In the previous decade, these questions inspired the fight for financial inclusion and the legacy that Keane and I built. Now, these questions are leading a revolution around the world.

HOW I DISCOVERED RECLAMATION

According to the *Oxford English Dictionary*, **reclamation** is "the process of claiming something back or of reasserting a right." In its definition, reclamation implies a return to wholeness. It points to something precious that was once ours, which was taken away by an individual, an organization, or even a system.

By taking back that thing, we embody our fullest selves through the identities and the communities that we belong to.

The first time I heard the word *reclamation*, I was at a digital detox retreat called Camp Reset. Created by eight co-founders, many of whom were entrepreneurs or CEOs, they desired to create a space for nourishment and play. In their personal lives, many of them were unable to disconnect from work mentally or emotionally.

More importantly, they noticed a world where adults yearned to connect deeply with one another. Where were these spaces in adulthood? A conversation has emerged post-pandemic about the disappearance of the **third space:** the space that is neither our home (first place) nor our workplace (second place), where people can congregate and connect in person. In the past, these spaces would be cafes, bars, libraries, gyms, theaters, malls, churches, and

184

more. However, given that remote work has become prominent, now work has bled into the third space as well, with *Forbes* reporting the future likelihood of using a third place for work (e.g. cafe, parks) at 98%.[14]

Why do I share this? Camp Reset was co-founded in 2015 and even back then, they were seeing a world without real talk. Empty, meaningless, superficial. Too focused on just work and success, without considerations and space being made for the human in all of us.

At my inaugural Camp Reset, 250 campers stepped off buses and were ushered into a large cafeteria. It was June 2017 and we were at Camp Wahanowin, an overnight camp away from the city. No Wi-Fi or electronics were allowed, and upon arriving, we gave our phones to the event organizers, who locked them away for the weekend.

It was in this cafeteria, surrounded by hundreds of strangers, that I heard a land acknowledgment for the first time: "We acknowledge the land we are meeting on is the traditional territory of many nations, including the Mississaugas of the Credit, the Anishnabeg, the Chippewa, the Haudenosaunee, and the Wendat peoples and is now home to many diverse First Nations, Inuit and Métis peoples."[15]

It was powerful.

It was the first time I heard sincere and compassionate remorse for the atrocities that had occurred. It was a statement that honored Indigenous people as the original stewards of the land. It acknowledged that colonialism and racism existed in physical, social, and emotional spaces. Furthermore, it didn't just stay as a statement or a thing to say: Camp Reset has continued to integrate practices, services, and products that showcase the work of Indigenous leaders, while extending it to other communities as well. In 2023, Reset launched a physical center inside the neighborhood of Little Jamaica, causing its co-founders to invite members of the Jamaican community to co-create their own sessions and to introduce their own artists into the center.

Confronting yet respectful, it started my journey around justice and its importance on moving the needle of workplace mental health.

There can be no healing without justice. In a world where systems have broken down, where conditions like depression and anxiety have skyrocketed, and where citizens of every level are discontent or even enraged, it is a cry for help. It is a call for leaders of leaders to guide us in these difficult times, especially in the workplace, where justice allows healing and well-being to last and to occur inside the systems we interact with.

At Camp Reset, a place that prided itself on play, it was essential that safety, respect, and inclusion were created across the community. Play, especially as adults, is a vulnerable practice. To ask people to lower their walls required intentionality from the facilitators.

Through their words and their actions, they showed that inclusion was not just a catchphrase but embedded in the fabric of community building.

Similar to our work at #REALTALK, we acknowledge the role that inequality and discrimination play in the experience of workplace mental health. It matters to the people we work with and the people who buy from us. We cannot create lasting change in mental health if the people we are empowering are stripped of their dignity, power, and expression as leaders.

In moving #REALTALK toward a collective Us, we restore the wholeness of the people we serve and work with, along with the communities they belong to.

It requires leaders creating leaders who can create meaningful impact across systems. What do we need to understand to bring #REALTALK with Us into the world?

THE MISSING PIECE

Writing this book has taken a significant amount of time – several years.

As a Founder and CEO, I was balancing between scaling my company and creating intentional space for this book. The day I knew this book needed to be written was the day we reached 40 000 leaders in impact.

This was a milestone in the number of tech leaders we had worked with, educating others through live events and live programming.

It should have been a happy moment, but instead, this milestone took the wind out of my sails.

We were three years into #REALTALK, and it felt like nothing had changed. Not at the industry level anyway. Even though we had the support of high-profile champions across North America, the stats on workplace mental health remained the same.

Founders were still experiencing depression, anxiety, and burnout in high numbers. It was also apparent that the most vulnerable populations, women and Black, Indigenous, and People of Color (BIPOC), were suffering the most. They still felt unsafe, constantly threatened, or triggered in an industry whose systems were resistant to transformation.

It was a year later, in my experiences of Black Lives Matter and #StopAsianHate, that I understood the missing piece – reclamation.

For so long, founders and leaders of leaders have fallen short of what is truly possible. Meaning well, our definition of combating sexism and racism has been "performative" in nature. In the world of Diversity, Equity, and Inclusion, an action is **performative** when it looks good (social capital) but has little impact on the actual or root cause (true activism).

In the instance of Women in Tech movements, which have been prevalent since the 2010s, they are marked by their large events and platforms. Communities by the thousands and even millions, like Sophia Amoruso's #girlboss, gather on stages and speak on the importance of women's representation in leadership and entrepreneurship.

What is rarely seen, yet needed, is "rocking the boat" – calling out unjust practices and taking the actions that move the needle on money and power.

For example, COVID-19 has demonstrated massive disappointment in tech's C-Suite leaders, one of the most affluent and influential groups in the world. Venture capital knows they have a diversity problem in their senior investment teams, which are 92% male and 78% white.[16] Leadership teams at major tech companies are 23% female and 77% male as well.

At a turning point on our planet, shaped by #MeToo, Black Lives Matter, and #StopAsianHate, tech's C-Suite leaders can lead the charge and create a better planet.

Instead, many tech leaders have responded to these issues by going back to what is comfortable, shrinking rather than expanding their leadership. In October 2020, Pitchbook reported: "Quarterly VC funding for female founders drops to a three-year low." They found the following:[17]

- Firms invested a total of $434 million in Q3, the lowest figure since Q2 2017.
- Q3 2020 is a 48% drop in funding for female founders from Q2 2020.
- Staying in the startup world is a chicken-and-egg problem, where economic uncertainty has led women to hold on to other jobs with income and health benefits.

Leslie Feinzaig, founder and CEO of the Female Founders Alliance, notes that, "This causes a vicious cycle: If women feel they can't raise capital successfully, they become more likely to scrap their entrepreneurial plans."

Thus, change cannot become transformation without a clear, non-negotiable stand toward a vision. Like r/wallstreetbets and crypto, where millions of citizens have aggregated and held the line, this conviction is essential for these times.

Where have all the brave ones gone?

HOW RECLAMATION TRANSFORMS US

When Keane passed away, it shifted my relationship with trauma.

I had spent so long trying to "heal" myself. I had completed my undergraduate and graduate degrees in social and developmental psychology. I had spent a decade working with therapists, counselors, and coaches to unravel my patterns and my wounds. I had been a renowned special education teacher, led a national movement in mental health, and was featured in *Forbes* and *Inc.* for my work.

It still felt tough.

It was not until later that I understood: trauma lives not just in our individual experiences but in what we experience as a collective. In being a witness to trauma, we experience its effects.

As a woman of color, it has felt like a long and uphill road to get here. I know many women can relate to the exhaustion of having to prove themselves, day in and day out, that our experiences and our expertise are valid. Where men are judged on their potential, women are judged on their experience.

Rather than being given an encouraging hand, we are asked to defend ourselves.

Every day, I am surrounded by an industry and a world where women are survivors of violence and harassment. In turning on the TV or the news, I am bombarded with confusing and demeaning messages about what it means to be Asian.

In witnessing trauma directed at others who look like me, we are affected.

This trauma perpetuates in our systems today, which fail to acknowledge the impact of cultural and intergenerational trauma. It means a daily experience of life where the norm is an erosion of our identity and our worth.

The most vulnerable experience psychological harm. They experience a crippling of self.

Healing our past is not enough. Not in a world where the status quo is the inequality and harm that exists in every space and in every interaction.

We need something different. We need reclamation.

For every instance where our self is eroded by another, we must reaffirm who we are. That has been the hardest and most inspirational part of

#REALTALK during COVID-19: to take a stand. In every space in which I speak, facilitate, or heal, I choose my story.

I choose a story of a woman of color, who embodies healing and justice in every space, who compassionately yet honestly points out inequality where I go. I choose the story of Cherry Rose Tan, who is more than a media bite about a sibling's death. I choose a story of a Filipino–Chinese Canadian, who calls forward my colleagues and my clients to stand alongside #StopAsianHate.

To break free of the old systems that bind us, we must reclaim our truth each day, and we must do so unapologetically. In October 2020, the song "Mother's Daughter" by Miley Cyrus became the rallying cry for the protests in Poland, where 100 000 people demanded the decriminalization of abortion. For Lil Nas X in March 2021, his song "Montero" was praised for being "unabashedly queer," expressing his sexuality as a gay man on an international stage.

As a leader of leaders, you can play a proactive part in your chosen mission by giving your people an opportunity to become leaders. It means that rather than throwing your people into the waters of innovation, hoping they will swim and not drown, you can support and prepare them instead. You can encourage a culture of **learning**, being diligent and proactive about what is really required to make that innovation occur. Unlike others that have failed, you can invest in the growth and empowerment of your people, so they receive the training and the skill set required to navigate these waters.

As a keynote speaker who is hired to speak on innovation and exponential technologies, I have to manage the expectations of those who hire me. I am upfront that my keynotes will inspire, educate, and create action, but that if they want to win the game of innovation, organizations will need to go much deeper to train and prepare their employees. A single keynote, done once a year, will not be enough for the workers of today (which includes us) to feel confident in executing that innovation in their day-to-day. It requires the ongoing resilience, willingness, and knowledge of your people to adapt.

To show you what this really means, we must understand how workplaces have often failed their people when it comes to preparing them for innovation. A 2022 article from Lorman, a global training solutions company serving over 1.4 million professionals, found the following:[18]

- Fifty-nine percent of employees had no workplace training and most of their skills were self-taught.
- Fifty percent of managers with over 10 years of experience have only received about 9 hours of training.
- Seventy-four percent of employees aren't reaching full potential due to lack of career development opportunities.
- Thirty-four percent of employees who left their previous job were motivated by more career development opportunities in their new role.
- Eighty-six percent of Millennials would re-consider leaving their current job if training and development were offered by their employer.

In an article written by Børge Brende, president of the World Economic Forum, he also noted that 54% of employees will require re-skilling and up-skilling to stay in their jobs, with 35% needing 6 months, 9% needing 6–12 months, and 10% needing more than a year to complete this training.[19]

As we think about creating a thriving workplace that persists in the face of innovation, we need to remember that innovation is a long-term game. A long-term game where leaders of leaders can harness the power of reclamation for themselves, their teams, and their organizations, so that the frustration and anger of people can be harnessed into doing good.

In choosing our truth each day, reclamation transforms and frees us. It paves a path for those like us to follow, to glimpse a different way to do and to be. By leading and creating alongside others at a systemwide level, we break the cycle for ourselves and our communities.

INTERNAL EXERCISE: THE OTHERED SELF

To reclaim something, we must understand which parts of ourselves we made "other." In sociology, **othering** is the process of assigning negative characteristics to other individuals or groups, deeming them as "alien" or "not us." This practice is used in power dynamics like politics, where othering divides and dehumanizes groups.[20]

This concept of othering occurs within ourselves too. In the tech industry, we have spent years or even decades "othering" parts of our identity away in order to survive. Ways of succeeding that require pretending and hiding, rather than being real. To create new systems, rather than incrementally improving the existing ones, requires a different type of person than the one that got us here.

Unlocking this leadership starts with our own reclamation.

Instructions:

1. **Identity:** Using the table below, fill out the first column. List the part(s) of your identity that you have resisted or made "other."
2. **Othering:** For each identity, complete row by row. Write down the ways in which you have separated yourself from this identity. What patterns exist in your behavior?
3. **Power:** When we experience resistance to something, it means our relationship with that thing involves emotions like frustration, guilt, and shame. Why have you chosen to "other" this identity? What are the areas of life where you are disempowered as a result?

4. **Embodiment:** To create new possibilities, we must make different choices. It means choosing day in and day out to embody that part of ourselves. By doing so, it becomes Being (a natural part of who we are) rather than Doing (a conscious practice or habit). What is the way(s) you can accept and embrace this part of yourself? How can you incorporate not just your mind or your heart, but your body into this practice?

Identity: What part of my identity have I othered?	Othering: How have I separated this part from myself?	Power: How and/or where does it hold power over me?	Embodiment: What action will I take to express this identity?
Parenthood	Resisting any conversation around children. Filling my time with work ("too busy for kids"), rather than taking time to reflect	Obligation and resentment because of my childhood. Heated conversations with current or past partners, e.g. being triggered	Creating space this year, to explore if I wish to be a dad. Having the conversation, free of my past and my trauma
Fun	Rejecting parts of my "old life," including former friends. Becoming incredibly serious and proper in my personal and professional life	Makes it difficult to accept gifts in relationships. Staying in my head by overthinking, causing me to disconnect from my body	Returning to my daily practices of self-care and play. Reducing my TV and junk food intake, to move away from numbing
French	Primarily consuming English-speaking shows or music. Rejecting traditions from my parents, rather than coming from curiosity	Embarrassment around not knowing my own customs or history. "Not belonging" when I travel to French-speaking areas	Enrolling in French classes to connect with my heritage. Reconnecting with older relatives in Quebec, to learn what it was like back home

EXTERNAL EXERCISE: YOUR PEOPLE

When we involve the community in our lives, real talk can create incredible results in our personal and professional lives. Identity is not an individual concept, but an understanding and listening of the person that is held by our family, friends, colleagues, and more.

Reclaiming ourselves as a lived reality requires our community. It means building a network of people who champion and support our possibility (Receive). At the same time, our journey impacts and lifts others who are like us (Give). We both receive and give by choosing to accept and embrace the communities we have long resisted.

In my life as a Woman of Color founder, I hold multiple, high-profile positions that inspire future women to enter entrepreneurship. Many of my fourth-year students at the Schulich School of Business are women who are learning about entrepreneurship for the first time. Most of them leave with a clarity of the causes or missions that move them, plus the ideas for their first business. How can you receive and give to your communities and your people?

Instructions:

1. **Identity:** Using the identities listed in the previous exercise, copy those words into the first column.
2. **Community:** For each identity, write down the name of one community that you can join. Be as specific as possible by listing an actual organization or group. It makes this work actionable and tangible.
3. **Receive:** As we reaffirm our new identity, our past tempts us with old stories that no longer align to who we are and what we value. Do not be a lone wolf. Like the way we have masterminds for business,

our possibility becomes real by sharing it. Who from the community is willing to support you as a mentor, advisor, or friend?

4. **Give:** In reentering this community, we lead and are led. How will you give back to this community, especially to others who are upcoming? This section invites an intentional practice to enact your leadership.

Identity: What part of my identity have I made other?	Community: What and/or where is this community? Please describe.	Receive: Who from this community is championing and supporting me?	Give: How will I be contributing to this community? Name one action.
Parenthood	Working Parents Canada	Rachel Windler, Scott Aaronson	Providing advice and support on managing caregiver burnout
Fun	Boston Social Nights	Phoebe Denning	Volunteering my time each month to help with in-person events
French	Francophones in America	Louis Bastien	Mentoring other Francophones who have moved to the United States

HOLDING THE LINE

Reclamation is about owning our voice and our power, including the parts of ourselves that we have made other. By reclaiming our stories and channeling them into a force for change, we create a new path for ourselves and the people we lead. We move away from old paradigms of struggle, frustration, and even rage, taking a stand and following through with powerful choices.

Reclamation and the game of innovation are intertwined. We are facing unprecedented levels of stress and uncertainty, which have and will continue to affect our employees, our customers, and future generations. It is in reclaiming ourselves that our wounds become gifts. Our yes becomes loud and unapologetic, calling forward others into their leadership.

It is leaders creating leaders, so that real talk no longer lives in an individual moment, but lives in the collective fabric held by our communities and our workplaces. In the next chapter, we will learn how to build systems that expand and strengthen this leadership so that we create a world that works for more people.

CHAPTER ELEVEN

SOVEREIGNTY

It was November 2023 and all I felt was a sense of calm. Total and complete silence.

I was in Portland, Oregon, walking downtown at night and just watching. Observing. Taking it all in. It felt like I had reached a release, a pinnacle of sorts.

It had been two years since I set out the vision and mission for my personal and professional life. It included my new theme for the decade (generational wealth) and who I wanted to impact and work with. I had so much clarity after years of building and leading #REALTALK, and what came through that work and my own healing was that I had a message to tell.

That this message could change so many lives, even the world, if I just committed to it.

I had spent the last year going through ordeal after ordeal in my life. A close family member had become unemployed, my dad was diagnosed with Stage 3 cancer, and my previous publisher had become insolvent. The circumstances of my life felt so messy, and yet deep down, I knew this would only make me stronger. That one day, I would have a story to share that would impact not just the tech founders I serve, but the leaders of leaders who are embarking on the game of innovation.

In walking the streets of Portland that night, I felt absolved. I felt complete. I felt like I had unlocked a new future for #REALTALK: not just for tech founders, but a universal message that every workplace needed to hear. A way to build the future of your organization without burning out along the way.

For the past year, I had been working with the team at Video Narrative. The owner Chris West (once my mentor and now a friend) runs the top branding agency for keynote speakers in North America. Many of his clients are Hall of Fame speakers, best-selling authors, and more, who speak on the biggest stages on the planet. I hired him after months of deliberation because I wanted to be held, seen, and supported in my new vision. I wanted to be pushed and to be held to a much higher standard in order to fulfill the mission that I was determined to complete.

Being in Portland, I did just that. I had spent a whole day filming with Chris and his team of videographers, and I felt teary thinking about the events that led me here. I could feel the work we were doing between my speaker reel, my new website, and my first book (the one you are experiencing right now) as the cumulation of something special.

Instead of #REALTALK living within me, now we could bring it to a broader audience. Imagine **leaders of leaders** across every organization and every vertical, who could learn about the frameworks and lessons that #REALTALK gained from working with 40 000 tech leaders. Imagine if we could empower every industry to thrive and innovate in messy times. Imagine what we could do with the right frameworks and the right teams.

In spending the last few years investing in the right mentors and building my body of work, I saw how things were evolving. I saw that we were making this transition and that I was no longer doing it alone. With my video team, my sales team, my book publisher, and my bureau partners, we were executing this possibility in the world.

We were freeing leaders of leaders from the same mistakes that myself, my brother, and my family once made. We were breaking the cycle.

THE AGE OF MISTRUST

Trust is a rare and sought-after commodity.

At #REALTALK, we rebuild trust with ourselves, with others, and finally, with our communities. The growing stats on mental illness and trauma are a reflection of a world that seems harsh and unrelenting. #REALTALK started from this place, where even the most successful founders felt alone, unable to share truthfully with others.

From a bird's-eye view, mistrust has seeped into every part of life from the individual to the system. During COVID-19, there were government lockdowns and vaccine hesitancy. Citizens have questioned their governments and officials, ignoring restrictions. Governments have responded with more restrictions in response, escalating the conflict.

In April 2021, CNBC reported vaccine passports at Duke, Brown, Cornell, Northeastern, and Notre Dame, making vaccination mandatory for students to attend university.[1] Despite the availability of COVID-19 vaccines in the United States, only 58% of parents and caregivers vaccinated their children. Furthermore, Black and Latino households were more skeptical of the vaccines because of the medical mistreatment they faced in the past.

Trust has eroded from our societal fabric.

With the advent of the Big Five (Amazon, Apple, Facebook, Google, and Microsoft), it has been a long time coming. Nothing feels safe with data scandals like Facebook–Cambridge Analytica, where Mark Zuckerberg testified in front of Congress.

Citizens feel powerless, their privacy and liberty under threat.

From 2017 to 2018, Americans' trust in media dropped from 47% to 42% and trust in government dropped 14%.[2] People no longer trust individuals and even governments to "do what is right."

With this mistrust, people have become desperate and angry. It has set the stage for global phenomena like **cancel culture**, an act of visible and punitive harm to an identified transgressor. Unlike ghosting and boycotting, canceling is more extreme where the canceler seeks to punish that individual.

In a world where people lack agency in nearly every arena of their life, including the personal and professional, we are moving toward polarization and outrage.

Why does this matter? For teams and organizations to succeed in the face of uncertainty, we need trust. Trust is the backbone that allows us to rally as a collective, and without it, our response to change is abysmal. Oak Engage, a company empowering workplaces through modern intranet, found that the employees' largest resistances to change are: mistrust in the organization (41%), lack of awareness around the reason for change (39%), and fear of the unknown (38%).[3] McKinsey has also found 70% of all change programs fail due to employee resistance and lack of support from management.[4]

Thus, leaders of leaders like ourselves need to embody an organizational culture of real talk by being forthcoming about what's working or not working. No one can rise to this occasion on their own, and playing the game of innovation requires significant time and resources, pooled together. Our ability to engender trust needs to start in the short term and to last in the long term, so that we can stay future-proof.

Without a safe space to collaborate as a company or even an industry, innovation and value creation are halted. People become siloed and in-groups and out-groups start to form, where we exclude others that don't look or think like us. Mistrust makes it very difficult to solve large and systemic problems, such as mental health and housing affordability, when they affect a diversity of stakeholders and require multidisciplinary efforts to solve them.

Systems cannot be changed at the level of Me.

Without #REALTALK with Us, our systems will continue to fail or break down. We have lost the humanity and the communication necessary to co-create as partners.

THE UNWORKABLE WORKPLACE

When we suppress problems, those problems escalate. Demonstrated by our first wave of #REALTALK champions, the most-cited source of failure (self-identified by a group of 50 founders) was avoidance.

Ignoring or denying the problem until it snowballed into a crisis.

As leaders of leaders, our actions have long-term and significant consequences. To demonstrate the horrifying impact of these consequences, there was a study done in the world of tech. In 2017, The Kapor Center released the Tech Leavers Study, a first-of-its-kind analysis of why people voluntarily leave jobs in tech.[5] In interviewing 2000 US adults, they discovered that:

- Seventy-eight percent of employees experienced unfair treatment, while 85% witnessed unfair treatment in their previous company.
- Unfairness or mistreatment at work was the most-cited reason for leaving, with 37% saying that unfair treatment was a major factor for their leaving.
- Sixty-nine percent would have stayed at their previous company if there was an improvement in management and leadership.
- Every employee who leaves a tech job costs an average of $144 000 to replace, which totals to $16 billion each year as an industry.

These numbers are staggering and have a direct effect on the bottom line. Not only are there grave implications from a financial standpoint, a lack of real talk at the community level brings ethical considerations. In 2021, Google lost two of its top AI researchers after the controversial firing of Dr. Timnit Gebru, a prominent expert in the field of AI.[6] As the co-leader of the Ethical AI team at Google, she was working on a paper about the dangers of large language models. Google asked her to retract her paper and to remove herself and four of the five co-authors.

She refused.

Ironically, Dr. Timnit Gebru was hired to help Google manage the bias, fairness, and responsibility of AI. When she engaged in real talk on these topics, especially as a Black female tech leader, she was fired from the company. The concerns she brought up have only heightened in an era of ChatGPT and generative AI, where AI and its decision-making is only as effective as the data it is provided during training. Bad data equals bad results, or even worse, biased results made faster.

In our globalized society, our employees, our customers, and our investors are watching.

Earlier in this book, I shared my passion for being an MBA professor at the Schulich School of Business. In this role, I have had the honor of working with the next generation of leaders (Gen Z) each and every day. The first generation native to smartphones, social media, and video shorts, my students tell me on a regular basis that they are afraid. Afraid that they will come out of university with skills that are irrelevant to securing jobs.

Even before they enter the workforce full-time, they are grappling with conversations on how to enter, compete, and win the game of innovation because the world around them is changing so rapidly. As a result, 72% of Gen Z believe that traditional career paths aren't applicable to them anymore and 84% rank "creator" as the most feasible career, followed by "entrepreneur" at 78%.[7]

How can we lead our organizations into the future so these workplaces can engage and retain current and future generations? People are demanding social responsibility alongside financial success as we come toward a reckoning. Thus, sovereignty (as this chapter is aptly named) is an important part of sustaining real talk at the community level. For the most influential of us, we are being called to embrace #REALTALK with Us, bringing other voices to the table.

At #REALTALK, we were once a movement. Five years later, we are dreaming bigger.

Starting the discussion is not enough, not when the status quo deepens the inequality gap and the suffering of the vulnerable. We must create safe and honest spaces long enough for meaningful action to occur. Systems will only shift from a collaborative effort by multiple stakeholders who are moving toward a common cause.

Each stakeholder, empowered to share expertise and take action, can become a sovereign player in this dynamic. Instead of being threatened or sabotaged by others at the table, we leverage and honor each other's experiences, strengths, and contributions.

SOVEREIGNTY IN PRACTICE

At #REALTALK, we define **sovereignty** as the power and responsibility of each person to exercise their identity, property, and participation.

In this book, #REALTALK Leadership moves from Chaos → Control → Calm → Creation. Through #REALTALK with Us, we move past complacency by experiencing emotions as valuable, conversations as deep, and relationships as profound. The end result is expanding our leadership beyond ourselves so that every stakeholder around us, including our employees, can become leaders themselves.

By doing so, we become the **leader of leaders** I have mentioned time and time again. In inspiring our people toward a collective mission or objective, our leadership is building the shared future.

Similar to Maslow's hierarchy of needs, we can **self-actualize**: to fulfill and step into our highest potential in the workplace and at home. This opportunity applies to ourselves, along with the employees, customers, and people we touch. Like the global dialog on COVID-19, people yearn to be more than expendable commodities or nameless automatons.

People wish to be valued and acknowledged in their personal and professional lives. They want to know that they matter.

In the world of human systems, such as social and political, sovereignty is growing. Systemic problems like economic inequality are rooted in structures of power, requiring time and effort for collective change. We can observe advancements in finance and other industries as examples of what is possible. Here are three types of sovereignty in practice:

1. **Crypto Sovereignty** is the power of each person to exercise their economic, social, and political rights through a digital, decentralized economy. To fulfill this vision, blockchain has created **self-sovereign identity (SSI)**, where people own and control their identity and their data without third-party entities.[8] Similar to real life, where we self-organize and participate with others, digital identity is becoming decentralized. The citizen, rather than the platform, owns their identity and its usage and data so that no citizen can have their identity stripped away by a single or arbitrary entity.

2. **Body Sovereignty** is the right of each person to have full autonomy of their body. In society, we are bombarded with messages about

what our body should look or feel like. In October 2020, Poland deemed "abortion in cases of severe and irreversible fetal abnormalities" as unconstitutional, representing 98% of their abortions.[9] Thus, body sovereignty rejects interference from third parties by advocating for complete body autonomy. There is no "right" way to have a body and each individual decides their level and form of participation.

3. **Food Sovereignty** is the right of each person "to healthy and culturally appropriate food produced through ecologically sound and sustainable methods, and their right to define their own food and agriculture systems."[10] At the 1996 World Food Summit, this term was introduced by La Via Campesina, an international farmers' movement of 182 organizations in 81 countries. It promotes justice and dignity within the agriculture industry, fighting against the injustice in the food system. Women produce 70% of the food worldwide, yet they continue to be financially disenfranchised in those regions.

As we expand our leadership, we can use our influence to elevate our communities. To move upward and to take people with us, as we become more successful ourselves. The inequality gap increased during COVID-19, with tech-based companies like Amazon, Tesla, and Microsoft receiving the majority of the spoils. Rather than continuing the traditions of unconscious capitalism, we can become intentional.

It is through sovereignty that we can ask ourselves, *Who are we? What does our leadership represent? What can we create as a community?* This chapter invites you to dream boldly, a leadership that inspires our full potential as Spaceship Earth, a term coined by Buckminster Fuller to imagine a thriving, resource-efficient planet for generations to come.

What is possible with this type of leadership?

RESILIENT, SMART DESIGN

In a world where our actions inspire individual and collective sovereignty, we move toward **resilient, smart design:** systems thinking that anticipates and addresses the multifaceted problems of today.

#REALTALK is focused on Founder Mental Health, yet our work incorporates the pillars of integrity, healing, and justice. We account for justice upfront because our clients, such as universities and accelerators, will have founders who are women and/or Black, Indigenous, and People of Color.

These discussions, often ecosystem- or community-based in nature, are inevitable in an increasingly globalized world.

Through resilient, smart design, we acknowledge the risk and mitigate the harm created by systemic barriers like racism and sexism. In our intention to empower all founders to be self-sovereign, self-organizing, and self-creating, we design systems that last across demographics, psychographics, and even values.

To make this possibility a reality, we must put in the work and move away from quick-fix solutions. Royal Bank of Canada, Canada's most valuable company, released a 2018 report called *The Coming Skills Revolution.* By 2030, they predict that 28% of Canadians will be foreign-born and 32% of Canadians will be visible minorities.[11] Noel Baldwin, Director of Government and Public Affairs at the Future Skills Centre, noted the following: "I don't think the world will get any less globalized, and the intercultural aspect of that will affect collaboration and working in teams."

As leaders of leaders, we can create leaders throughout our organization rather than victims, martyrs, or dependents.

By embracing diverse thinking, we can enhance innovation by 20% and reduce risk by 30%.[12] From my two decades of lived trauma, I have become a better builder for myself and my industry. As a Filipino-Chinese woman and a first-generation immigrant, I have experienced danger (physical harm) and fear (psychological threat) in a variety of personal and professional contexts.

It is these experiences that inform my gifts for harm reduction and risk mitigation with founders. It is these experiences that allow tech CEOs from all walks of life, including White men, to feel safe and seen in the spaces that I create.

At #REALTALK, we anticipate these difficult topics to appear and we plan for it ahead of time. We create agreements and spaces at every level, from the investor to the founder, *before* we start a conversation. We practice nonviolent communication with every client to reduce emotional harm. We ask for permission before delving into sensitive topics so that clients can voice their boundaries and their needs.

These practices were initially made to support the marginalized and the vulnerable, yet they lift all boats. These practices form a resilient, smart design and better serve every founder that enters our space.

As you integrate sovereignty into your leadership, I invite you to flip the script. These uncomfortable yet timely conversations (real talk) can be the untapped opportunity for our companies. In leaning into #REALTALK with Us, we can transform our systems and deepen our bottom line.

YOUR CIRCLE OF TEACHERS

In order to implement sovereignty, a mechanism for building leaders around you at scale, we need to build a strong and robust network of teachers. Even the most talented of leaders cannot execute on systems design, transformation, or innovation alone. It means we need the right advice and resources from the right people at the right time. Venture capital has continued to punch above its weight in terms of job creation and value creation because of our discernment and structure around mentorship.

In the world of startups, there are three types of teachers out there, which should be vetted and recruited to your inner circles:

1. **Coaches** are professionals who are trained to ask powerful questions, in order to solicit different ways of thinking and to draw out leadership skills from the individual. Having a coach is a more formal structure, often with a set amount of hours (e.g. 1 hour per week for six months) and a predetermined fee. There are coaches who are more generalized (e.g. business) and coaches who are more specialized (e.g. B2B sales).

2. **Mentors** are individuals further ahead in their career path, who share perspective, experiences, and introductions to support their mentee's journey. These mentors are motivated by more than money, where the structure is informal, such as being accessible by cell phone or email and with no defined hours or fee. Mentors benefit from this relationship by having a pulse on what's new and leaving a legacy through their mentees.

3. **Advisors** are veterans who have built the thing you are asking about (e.g. YouTube channel, SaaS startup), where they have a defined track record in the deliverable or venture you are looking to execute on. In the startup space, this means founders who have previously raised VC money or exited their company through IPO, acquisition, and more. Startups rely on advisors the most, out of the three classes we just described.

At Schulich, I teach three MBA-level Entrepreneurship courses and my favorite course is called Intelligent Innovation Ecosystem Design. A special course, half of my students are domestic from Schulich, while the other half are exchange students from Germany, Singapore, New Zealand, Peru,

Israel, and more. In this course, I teach the full life cycle of startups from inception to exit, with the purpose of creating **unicorns** (companies valued at $1B or more). We study the history of large startup ecosystems (cities) around the world, who have a track record of producing not just one, but multiple unicorns.

In the startup world, there is a pattern of de-risking and success called the **PayPal mafia:** startups who have at least one employee/co-founder who previously worked at a unicorn will have a higher chance at success.[13] It derives its name from the results created by the early team of PayPal, who have been responsible for many of the startup unicorns in America, such as Elon Musk (Tesla, SpaceX), Reid Hoffman (LinkedIn, Greylock), Jeremy Stoppelman and Russel Simmons (Yelp), Chad Hurley, Steve Chen, and Jawed Karim (YouTube), Peter Thiel (Palantir, Founders Fund), and Keith Rabois (Square).

This is a such an important pattern that entire VC firms will base their investment strategy on finding these individuals, even hosting private events to network with talent from Square, Meta, Uber, and more *before* they leave the company. Startups also try to obtain this talent as co-founders, early employees, or advisors in exchange for equity, money, or both.

When we think about creating systems change through #REALTALK with Us, we need to strategize our **advisory mix:** the specific combination of coaches, mentors, and advisors that give us the best shot at navigating the game of innovation. The distribution of these types of teachers will shift depending on your circumstances and what stage you are at as a company.

For instance, early-stage founders benefit greatly from advisors and mentors but are less served by coaches because they need access to specific domain or technical expertise. On the other hand, late-stage founders are integrating all three types, where coaches become beneficial as a way to increase the leadership performance of themselves, their teams, and their organizations. As previously mentioned, a great example is Canadian unicorn Shopify, where they have a team of on-staff coaches who train middle and upper management, plus a defined structure on who and when people can access this leadership support.

In building this circle of teachers around us, we move away from micromanaging. We begin to create leaders, are supported in our own leadership, and can even delegate non-essential functions, in order to unlock more capacity and performance. As a recovering Type A, leaders of leaders often get to where they are by hustling or working very hard. This means taking on many or most of the components of the business.

However, as the business scales, we need to build a team of leaders and teachers around us.

For myself, my advisory mix was key in having my most successful year in business. While scaling my personal brand as an innovation and mental health speaker, I was in the middle of launching a nationwide initiative called Schulich Venture Academy (SVA). It was a stressful deliverable in partnership with four prominent C-Suite leaders, all of whom lead or invest in unicorn companies, and we hit 115% of our sales target in two months. Not only were we able to achieve this result with limited resources and a short runway, but I hadn't led a single sales call. My entire team handled sales because I had hired a former head of sales from a Series A startup, who was already in the ecosystem and had extensive experience with startup sales.

As a result, I was able to focus on what I do best: training leaders of leaders like my head of sales and handling strategic partnerships, while my head of sales was in the day-to-day work of executing those sales calls. What could you truly unlock as an organization if you had a circle of leaders and teachers with you, all in service to the one vision or mission you have declared?

The sky is the limit here.

A FRANK CONVERSATION ON ACCESS AND POWER

Before we enter into our practical exercises, I want to address the elephant in the room: access and power and how they come hand-in-hand. As a leader of leaders, I pride myself on being optimistic and inspiring, but also firm and tactical.

As you continue to bring real talk into the workplace and into your communities, access and power will come into play. **Access** is your ability to enter into spaces or conversations where the most resources or influence reside, in order to move from linear to exponential results. **Power** is the level of influence you already have, such as social or financial, based on your personal and professional background.

It goes without saying that the more access and power you have, the more potent your actions become on creating results. Especially oversized or unexpected results, like punching above your weight. This consideration is especially important in these times, when companies are looking to cut costs and yet hinge their success on their ability to unlock their people's best work.

If you wish to lead and create tangible impact, we must acknowledge the access and power we currently have and what we need to get there. As a woman of color, I know this conversation is uncomfortable and many spaces dance around this topic, rather than address it head-on. As you grow your circles, it is critical to invite individuals that are alike (look or think like you) and individuals that are different. When I mentor women founders, I tell them that it is tempting yet limiting to only hang out in women-centric founder or investor communities.

It is my deepest belief that we reduce our access and our power when we are in homogenous groups or spaces, and I have seen this play out in terms of professional results. In my work at Schulich Startups, I made an intentional choice to co-lead this ecosystem with a White man. It was important to me because I knew that there were spaces or conversations (e.g. poker tables, sailing invitations) where he would be welcome, where I would not. At the same time, I had access to different spaces or conversations that he needed to understand or know, such as women and Gen Z.

In us partnering together in this way, we created incredible results that neither of us could have achieved alone. Twice the network, twice the resources, and efficient in its lack of redundancy too. It was similar to how Keane and I partnered with another co-founding family, one from a different cultural and racial background than us, so that we could build relationships with banks, governments, and other stakeholders to tackle global remittance.

When you think about creating leaders of leaders across your organization or community, how are you making sure that access and power have been addressed? How are you assessing and clearing your biases, in order to maximize the utility of your existing networks? Which opportunities or partnerships can you say "yes" to today, in order to expedite this process?

One of the latest plays I have made in the professional realm is networking and partnering with creators, like YouTubers and TikTokers. As someone who started my founder journey in the edtech space, I have told investors that the future of education is heading toward short-form video, microlearning, and the ability to work with trusted, niche experts. Why learn from an institution you don't know, when you can learn from your favorite creator whose content you've consumed for years?

In realizing this trend, I have spent the last year co-founding with Glenys Omenya, a Black Gen Z creator who has grown her channels organically to 1.1 million followers. We were introduced by mutual friends and we've partnered together to create One Percent-Her, a global entrepreneurial movement for Gen Z and Millennial women. These channels, which were unbranded and are now part of our company, inspire women around the world with daily video content. Our bold vision is to empower millions of women to build their wealth, brand, and lifestyle, to carve a legacy on their terms.

I have invested a considerable amount of time and money into this endeavor, knowing that partnering with someone so different from me would open a new level of access and power in my life. What could I do and share with a starting audience of over a million people? What impact could I create in learning from a successful creator, who is a master in making things go viral? What could we do together, in partnering together and contributing such different skillsets?

As you think about unlocking a different level of performance through #REALTALK with Us, lean into the different. The weird. The polarizing. Think carefully about the stakeholders you are engaging with, the possibilities that different combinations can create, and how access and/or power will be key in achieving the results and impact that you desire.

INTERNAL EXERCISE: NORTH STAR

Sovereignty is the energy of fire and rebellion for a cause, a healthy form of anarchy. As you take a stand and create leaders alongside you, destruction and creation will occur. Sovereignty requires saying no to everything else, while saying yes to the one thing that matters.

In making this transition, it can be easy to lose your way.

Often, the most inspiring examples of sovereignty happen in the most desperate and restrictive of times. Movements like crypto, #MeToo, and Black Lives Matter have inspired generations because of their difficult, yet brave stance in the face of nonagreement. In being a leader, we must stay grounded and create an internal anchor to guide us.

In this exercise, you will be exploring a concept called the North Star. Like an anchor in the night sky, this landmark will guide you at all times.

It is a single word that encompasses *who* you want to be as a leader: the embodiment of your words, thoughts, and actions.

Whenever you are lost, you can see your North Star and be pointed in the right direction.

Instructions:

1. **Exploration:** A North Star is a characteristic or a value that declares who we are as a possibility. It is a function of Being, not Doing. We focus on *who* we are because it informs every decision we make. It provides direction as leaders of leaders, without controlling and worrying about every action. Write down the words that come to you. Release your judgment and be open to what shows up.

2. **Feeling:** Once you have the list, read each word aloud. For each word, allow it to settle into your body. Notice how it feels. What sensations are you feeling? Which word(s) excites or scares you?

3. **Resonance:** Read the list aloud a second time. Begin to cross out the words that are a no or even a lukewarm yes. Repeat this step, eliminating words until you are left with a single, remaining word. This word is your North Star.

4. **Anchor:** When self-work is engaging with *who* we are (Being) or what we do (Doing), we can fall into old patterns or identities. Our North Star is often a stretch for us, making us uncomfortable and creating growth as a result. We can strengthen this North Star in our lives by creating practices that anchor this word into our identity and our behavior.

Examples of Anchors:

- **Visual Reminders:** My previous North Stars were Greatness, Grace, and Ease. Each of those years, those traits were missing in my life.

To remember each word, I wrote my North Star on every journal and phone cover, strengthening my connection to it.

- **Leaders List:** To make this North Star more tangible, research other leaders who embody this characteristic or value. Write a list of those names on a piece of paper, which you can carry and read each day.
- **Recorded Affirmations:** Write an affirmation or mantra, expressing your commitment to this value and the thoughts, feelings, and behaviors you want to embody. You can record this affirmation on your phone, and listen to it each morning.

EXTERNAL EXERCISE: CALLING FORWARD

Sovereignty represents the ability to self-organize and self-select the way we express and participate. For #REALTALK with Us, our expression of who we are and what we stand for catalyzes those around us. In building a world that works for everyone, we need our stand to live in our communities and to exist outside of our individual, day-to-day actions.

In writing this book, we have done so with #REALTALK. This possibility is no longer about my brother's death or about our team, but about something much greater.

Combined with sovereignty, we create leaders who take the possibility of workplace mental health much further than what we could have done alone. We need as many people on board (e.g. founders, leaders of leaders, partners) to break the cycle of burnout, overwork, and apathy in the workplace.

Instructions:

1. **Community:** Review your exercises from the last chapter. From your completed homework, select one community that you would like to transform. A community is a specific group or organization that you can impact. You should be able to identify the people in that community.

2. **Stand:** With your North Star, select a stand that you are creating with that community. A **stand** is a vision of the future that stakeholders can rally upon, stating these results as tangibly as possible. For example, our stand at #REALTALK is that founders deserve to be fully seen and supported so that entrepreneurship can heal and transform the world.

3. **People:** Who are three people in this community who would build this stand with you? If you were assembling a "co-founding team," who would it be and why? List those three names. These individuals can be advisors, peers, or mentees (e.g. team members), whose leadership you want to see grow.

4. **Invitation:** For each individual, brainstorm the role they could have. When we engage people in #REALTALK with Us, we are calling people forward into a shared vision. What are the gifts they bring or the responsibilities available to them? How can you create a win-win and support each other?

5. **Action:** Call each of the individuals on your list. Have a "real talk" about what you see for the community and for them. How would you like them to be involved? What are they communicating back to you? What do they need in order to be a yes?

Community: VC Unlocked by 500 Global

Stand: Founders deserve to be fully seen and supported so that entrepreneurship can heal and transform the world.

People	Invitation: What do I see in them? What is their role in this stand or possibility?
Arlan Hamilton, Managing Partner at Backstage Capital	Has broken the glass ceiling in VC (e.g. Black, lesbian, woman), as the managing partner of her own firm Similar to #REALTALK, she works inside the system by gathering and creating with power players Can partner together on flipping the script and framing underrepresented founders as the next big opportunity
Pocket Sun, Managing Partner at SoGal Ventures	Has advocated for mental health and supports the next generation of founders Operates a program called Build Without Burnout, a six-month founder wellness program Can be a champion for Gen Z and Millennials by moving the needle on founder mental health

MOVING FORWARD, TOGETHER

As we complete our journey with #REALTALK with Us, I thank you for your commitment to doing the work. The deep work. The messy work. As leaders of leaders, our people and our organizations look at us to lead. In a post-COVID world, we can be a force for disproportionate good, leading from a place that supports mental health, systems thinking, and the well-being of more people.

We are becoming more globalized and more polarized, and we will need leaders to step up and unite us. As Andrew Yang, a former US presidential candidate once said, "It is not left, it is not right, it is forward."

That is what #REALTALK is all about. Leaders creating leaders, honoring the sovereignty of individuals and communities, as we create new systems for ourselves and future generations to come.

CHAPTER TWELVE

BEING THE BRIDGE

It is March 2024 and my life has come full circle.

I am standing on a large stage, in front of a beautiful atrium with impossibly tall ceilings and an audience of future leaders listening. To my left is a large sign that says "LEAD," a reminder to myself to continue the journey I started with Keane all those years ago.

This is me that day. I will always remember the importance of speaking our truth and embodying real talk.

I had spent the day surrounded by an incredible team: my makeup artist, my videographers, my social media manager, and the event organizers. My heart felt so full, feeling and knowing that I was fully supported as a leader of leaders. Between my work as an innovation and mental health speaker, Schulich Startups, and my new company, One Percent-Her, my vision was held and being built by 40 team members and student volunteers.

It was incredible.

What impacted me the most was realizing how universal, how relatable, the messages of #REALTALK were. I was hired to be the closing speaker for Toronto Metropolitan University, a major university here in Canada, on the eve of their 10-year conference anniversary. Ten years since they started organizing this flagship student leadership conference, serving thousands of students in their career journeys.

In speaking with these students about the losses I experienced, the creation of #REALTALK as a result, and the deeply personal and professional lessons I had to impart, I felt complete. Despite the worries I had the last month, wondering if they were ready to hear this message, I was wrong. They were more than ready and not only that: they needed to hear it.

From the organizers that day to the various attendees in the room, so many people came up to me to share how I changed their lives. They were grappling with their own fears and yet the stories and frameworks I taught gave them a way through. A glimpse of light in the darkness.

It was incredible to see the aliveness, the fire, in the room. So many of them reminded me of Keane back in his university days, eager and driven to be the change in the world. In speaking in front of them, I was moved to address them over and over again as "leaders."

Not students, not kids, but the leaders of their schools, their work-places, and the world.

It is no secret how passionate I am about the work we do at #REALTALK because I have lived it. I have lived through the pain of not having real talk, and what it cost me, my family, and my industry to have the conversation too late. Of what it costs us when we pursue success, without the mindset, heartset, and skillset to help us thrive and innovate in a messy world.

In pursuing and scaling this next evolution of my work, I feel grateful. Every day, I think about Keane in what I do and how I do it. I am still the same person I was all those years ago, pure and strong in mission. Yet at the same time, I am more powerful than ever, knowing that my challenges (and my victories) have given me the skills needed to truly impact this world at a different level.

As I think about the division and the suffering in this world, I am over-come by a sense of hope. A hope that we can find our way back to building the bridges toward understanding, collaboration, and peace.

A WORLD
WITH #REALTALK

At the start of our journey together, I shared one key message: that real talk is a necessary condition of leadership.

Similar to how 9/11 changed the world, COVID-19 has changed entire industries and communities. People have lost businesses, relationships, and lives, with deaths surpassing three million worldwide. With the global backdrop of #MeToo, Black Lives Matter, and now the recession, conversations like mental health and the future of work are here to stay.

At #REALTALK, our team has been honored to have served 40 000 leaders through live events. Being at the intersection of tech founders and mental health, we have been privy to the most vulnerable and intimate conversations on the planet. Founders sharing about depression, addiction, grief, and more, while holding very public and high-pressure roles, where hundreds and even thousands of people depend on them for their livelihood. Despite the material successes, I know my industry has slid back on factors like mental well-being and employee engagement.

The fact is, true leadership reveals itself in the face of crisis.

COVID-19 has shown us which leaders expand and which leaders shrink. Other historic events, from wars to famine, have done the same in human history. The systemic problems (and their solutions) will only amplify in importance as younger generations populate our workforce. Like the 2030 UN Sustainable Development Goals, leaders are rallying the planet toward a shared future of peace and prosperity for all people.

Our old systems are breaking down and are being challenged by the masses. In the face of this flashpoint, it is an opportunity for new paradigms and for bringing together every stakeholder for system-level transformation.

You can be the one to lead this.

Time and time again, we have seen the power that real talk grants in our personal and professional lives. Being able to process and complete trauma. Healing entire generations from hurt, violence, and more. Creating deeper connections with the people we love. Reclaiming our identity, along with the gifts it unlocks. Real talk is the building block for modern leadership, allowing us to tactically and compassionately address problems of any scale. Real talk is the gateway to innovating and thriving, while making sure the costs we pay (e.g. financially, mentally, emotionally) are within reason.

Real talk is resilient, smart leadership in the face of chaos.

A CULTURE OF COLLECTIVE OWNERSHIP

As you continue your path as a leader of leaders, I want you to remember that you are the bridge. You are the one that can empower people of all levels to take ownership of their professional lives, as we build toward a shared objective. In scaling real talk, it means creating leaders around us and building a culture of ownership and communication, where each individual feels like a meaningful part of the change being proposed.

No longer is it enough for leaders of leaders to send emails or decks, hoping that innovation will just run itself. We need to create a culture where we own the who, when, and why of what we do:

Who

The first piece in building a culture of ownership is the **who.** Who is the one that is responsible for implementing this strategy and/or innovation in the day-to-day? Is it the same person as the one who is responsible for the end result? Who are all of the different stakeholders involved, and what motivates each of them in the short term and the long term?

These are the questions we must answer to bring people together. A leader of leaders is not micromanaging their people, but inspiring them to become leaders themselves in the way they show up for themselves and others, especially when we aren't in the room. Regardless of their role and who they report to, each individual should see their role in the bigger mission or objective and what's in it for them.

The other piece about ownership is the art of **role creation**, making sure to define and to assign each responsibility to a particular individual, and for that individual to understand what success looks like in that defined role. When I coach startup teams, it is one of the first things we talk about. Investors often tell first-time founders that the composition and clarity of their founder team really matter. If you have co-founded a company with your best friend or a work colleague, and both of you have the same skillsets and plan on doing the same things, that creates confusion at the company: confusion in terms of who owns what and who is responsible for that function when it works or doesn't work.

In co-founding my latest company One Percent-Her (after being a solo founder for many years), my now co-founder and I had six months of conversations on our roles, the titles, and what success looked like qualitatively and quantitatively, in order to unlock certain benefits that we both agreed to. We sequenced a series of calls over those months, starting with calls about what we brought to the table and what we wanted out of a co-founding relationship. It was followed by calls on the deliverables we needed to launch this company, how we wanted to make money, what function(s) each individual was in charge of, and who they would need in their current or future team.

The end result of these conversations was a strong and respectful co-founding relationship, where I got asked to take on the chief executive officer (CEO) role, in charge of leading our business development and monetization strategies. My co-founder Glenys Omenya, who I mentioned earlier in this book, took on the title of chief creative officer (CCO). Both of us studied the composition of media-focused companies, especially creators with at least five million followers, and we felt this title encompassed her responsibilities of producing and editing content, while allowing her to grow into more marketing-centric responsibilities in the future.

In the startup world, we delineate these roles and responsibilities in writing, often in organizational charts (shown visually like a mind map) and also shareholder agreements when founder teams are made and compensated with present and future equity stakes. It can even include clauses around performance (specific to that person's function), in order to unlock more equity.

In sharing this example, how can you be more intentional about who is executing on what and the people and skillsets around them? Where do the opportunities lie in helping your people own their responsibilities and also their victories, so that the most ambitious leaders can rise?

It is an important consideration to think about, given the high performance required to create innovation and to protect your well-being.

When

The second piece in creating a culture of ownership is the **when.** When people hear this, many leaders default to thinking about the deadline. However, there is so much more that we can utilize to empower our people not just to start, but to finish their commitments. In the world of innovation, there is a massive problem right now in getting companies to that finish line, where many companies will announce a new innovation strategy (often top-down), only to pause or reverse that decision several months later.

The implications of this are severe, where employees become demoralized and mistrust in their leaders in the future. Good luck in getting your people on board the next time you announce a strategy!

In speaking of the when, we must maintain an executional timing that creates short-term wins *and* long-term wins. Remember that in my world of venture capital, which has played the game of innovation since the 1940s, our time horizon is 10–12 years per startup. Thus, we need a culture that can keep our people going through the good times and the bad.

Short-term wins allow our team to collect the small victories necessary to feel motivated, to feel capable, and to see that progress being made, creating the foundation of a resilient and motivated workplace. On the other hand, **long-term wins** keep the bigger vision in mind, creating significance and meaning in the work we are doing and all the people we will impact. Balancing these two dynamics is what helps us stay committed and in action as individuals and as a collective.

In my recent work launching Schulich Venture Academy (SVA), we balanced both types of wins. Our mission for the decade is to build the scale-up layer across Canada, so that Canada can compete on a global level. SVA took us 2.5 years to launch, where I led 20 people who we were part of this initiative. It included teams around Curriculum Design, Business Development, Sales, Marketing, Legal, Finance, and more, on top of managing relationships with external stakeholders like founder, venture, and ecosystem partners. Even though it was an incredibly intense launch, I continued to motivate our teams by creating a shared practice of weekly updates on Monday, weekly calls on Wednesdays for touch-ups and requests, and weekly wins on Fridays to acknowledge the contributions of each team member.

We also split our team into different specialities, where our more senior leaders (like myself) were in charge of maintaining the long-term pace (the vision), while empowering our direct reports (like my head of sales) to lead the short-term pace and their own teams. I worked with my direct reports on their leadership skills and internal systems as well, teaching them how to handle weekly calls, how to address setbacks from their own direct reports, and how to give feedback immediately and effectively. By having this balance, our teams felt like they were creating meaningful change (even in the earliest parts of our journey), while staying high performing to make this business a reality.

As you think about innovating and thriving as an organization, how are you balancing both of these timings as a leader of leaders? How are you creating wins and momentum within a weekly, monthly, quarterly, and even yearly time scale? An important and understated piece to consider.

Why

The last piece to building a culture of ownership is the **why**, the sense of purpose and the larger vision behind what we are building together. Many workplaces are going through a cultural and generational reckoning, where Gen Z have entered the workplace, Millennials have become the largest generation in the workplace, and Boomers are retiring.

Korn Ferry, one of the largest executive search firms in the world, published a 2015 report stating that Millennials want to work for **innovators**, companies who create groundbreaking products and services that actually improve the communities or customers they serve.[1] Millennials are a socially conscious generation and there is a distaste in working for companies who are seen as "profiteers" or "empire builders."

The upcoming generations want and demand more from their workplaces. They want to be engaged in their work, while doing good at the same time.

Recently, I did a keynote about this topic to a room full of CEOs and policymakers, as we discussed the future of Canada's economy and the entrepreneurial layer in our country. When a company creates the feeling of an individual why and also a collective why, they are able to develop more engaged and productive employees. An **individual why** is the significance or purpose of an employee's work on their own life, and how it moves forward the personal and/or professional goals they have.

When I got recruited to join Schulich, my colleague and co-leader, Chris Carder, did a fantastic job at this. I was not looking for another role because I was leading #REALTALK, but as we got to know each other, he understood that what motivated me as a person is empowering the next generation. It is an individual why I have held for many decades, stemming from my experiences in childhood. In Chris understanding this, he showed me how getting involved with Schulich could only amplify my individual why, by giving me a larger platform for my work and direct access to the younger generation.

At the same time, us leaders of leaders can steer the conversation on the **collective why,** sharing with our team(s) the vision for this company and what we stand for. To hold a collective why for a sustained period of time, it means embodying "real talk" in how you show up as a leader, where there is authenticity, courage, and commitment in that vision. At Schulich and even my work with #REALTALK, this has been one of my strengths: being a first mover, painting a picture of the movement we are creating together (even in its infancy), and helping people feel like they are the leaders, contributors, and champions of the mission.

#REALTALK as a company and as a movement was built in balancing these two types of why, where each #REALTALK Champion had their own reason for pledging their mental health story. Many of them were survivors themselves (individuals who had experienced mental illness, burnout, or trauma), but others were allies, who had been impacted by the experiences of loved ones or colleagues. What rallied us together as a collective was breaking the cycle for current and future founders, so that they could continue being in the ecosystem for years to come.

THE IMPACT THAT LIVES

As we wrap up this book, I want to share with you a moment that changed my life. A reminder that **this work matters.**

Many years ago, at the start of #REALTALK, I felt lost.

Every day was a struggle. I was recovering from a car accident, dealing with my brother's passing, and managing my mum's cancer. It was intense and scary, and I was suffering – badly. I couldn't pretend everything was okay. What I was experiencing was not something I could handle alone.

The turning point in my journey started with a company called TribalScale, an innovation firm that helps enterprises create digital products. Its CEO Sheetal Jaitly is a charismatic tech founder and community builder from Toronto. Keane and his co-founder were friends of Sheetal, having been colleagues at a previous company.

When Keane passed away, what touched me was how TribalScale and the broader tech community showed up for my family. They built a Google Drive to share news of Keane's passing, arranging for friends and colleagues to contribute their favorite pictures and videos of him. They assigned and coordinated roles as a community so that I wasn't organizing the funeral alone. They created the flyers for the funeral, sending invitations and reaching out to Keane's old network.

It was because of their efforts that 400 people attended Keane's funeral from over 10 different countries.

It was beautiful, daring, and amazing in its own way.

His funeral was like a national tech conference; the most influential leaders in tech and finance were there in attendance, paying tribute to Keane's life.

A few months later, I found myself on the high floor of a large commercial building in downtown Toronto. I was invited by two tech founders, who wanted to ask what they could do to help my Founder Mental Health cause. At the lobby where I checked in, something unexpected happened. A well-dressed man ran up to me and asked if I knew Keane. *That was bold,* I thought. *Who is this guy?*

I didn't know who this person was. I replied that Keane was my brother, and a magical conversation happened.

Edward (pseudonym) was a senior leader in our city, active in the tech ecosystem. He recognized me from the funeral. Edward wanted me to know that Keane changed his life and he would never forget it.

When Keane started in tech, Edward had a flourishing career in professional services. Keane pulled him aside one day and had a real talk with him. My brother knew that Edward was meant for something else.

That conversation changed the trajectory of Edward's life, where he left his previous employer and transitioned into tech.

It was because of that one conversation that Edward and I ended up meeting in that hallway years later, talking about the impact Keane had on both of our lives.

Since creating #REALTALK, I have experienced several conversations like this. When I speak at tech conferences, strangers approach me to share what Keane meant to them. When I visit accelerators and banks, executives say Keane's leadership inspired them.

Keane was so young, only 26 years old when he passed, yet his legacy lives on.

Every day, I miss Keane's presence in the world. I miss him as his sister. I miss him as part of two sibling entrepreneurs, who were daring to change the world.

In publishing this book, I feel complete with Keane's death. I wake up every day knowing that his legacy lives in our blockchain company and in small yet significant moments with other founders and leaders across the planet.

In Keane being an inspiration to others through real talk, I carry a love and devotion for our future leaders. We are at a turning point on the planet, where our friends and our neighbors are hurting. Through Keane's example and the thousands of real talks since, I believe in the possibility and transformation that we, as leaders of leaders, can bring to humanity.

May real talk transform you, your life, and your world in the most remarkable of ways. Thank you for sharing this journey with me. From one leader to another, I celebrate you.

CHAPTER SUMMARIES

Our journey has taken 12 chapters, 9 of which support the #REALTALK Leadership model. A book can be a lot to process.

Made for leaders of leaders like yourself, we prioritize execution over theory. We can spend months or years planning, but at the end of the day, results come from taking action.

To make these steps manageable, we have created Chapter Summaries to review the major concepts:

Conversation	Chapter	Takeaway
	Why #REALTALK	It is time to see this book in the hands of every leader, and for them to know they are not alone.
	Brave New World	Real talk is a necessary condition of leadership.
#REALTALK with Me	Stability	Stability is building the foundation for sustainable leadership.
	Integrity	Integrity is being real as leaders, rather than being right.
	Workability	Workability is restoring function in our personal and professional lives.
#REALTALK with You	Awareness	Awareness is labeling our emotions, to understand their influence on us.
	Compassion	Compassion is embracing, rather than rejecting, our emotions.
	Forgiveness	Forgiveness is completing the past, in order to create space for the future.
#REALTALK with Us	Identity	Identity is understanding who we are and where we have come from.
	Reclamation	Reclamation is owning the parts of ourselves we have made other.
	Sovereignty	Sovereignty is creating leaders around you, mobilizing toward a shared vision.
	Being the Bridge	In scaling real talk from Me to You to Us, that is how we as leaders thrive and innovate in a messy world.

#REALTALK with Me

Result: Chaos → Control

This part or Conversation addresses the **Mind (Thoughts)** using three steps: Stability → Integrity → Workability. All deep work starts with a real conversation with yourself. Without this foundation, transformation becomes unsustainable. Leaders often go from 0 to 100, leading to mental, emotional, or physical breakdowns as they scale their organizations. With #REALTALK with Me, we restore your sense of safety and resilience, creating functionality in eight areas of your life. Through rigorous self-care, we begin to shift from reacting (fear-based action) to responding.

The result is Chaos → Control. Most leaders start at Chaos, where leadership is putting out fires (Survive). Like Maslow's hierarchy of needs, the leader is focusing on survival and leaving themselves exhausted or disempowered. Leaders often start from this place.

In implementing #REALTALK with Me, we access Control: creating some autonomy and choice in our lives and in our businesses. This path is achieved through hard work, which feels effortful rather than intuitive, so **leadership is responding in the moment (Cope).** At this level, leadership occurs as **tolerable, shallow, and acceptable.**

#REALTALK with You

Result: Control → Calm

This part or Conversation addresses the **Heart (Emotions)** using three steps: Awareness → Compassion → Forgiveness. Self-help usually falls short by focusing on learning rather than application. The power of real talk lies in having real conversations with the most important people in our lives, like our family and our colleagues. At this level, we build our emotional muscles to accept, process, and embrace the emotions we usually avoid (e.g. anger, sadness).

We also understand the rarity and importance of completion: releasing the hold of the past, so we have space to think and create as leaders. It requires forgiving ourselves and others. Forgiveness is not condoning the past, but making the choice to move on.

The result is Control → Calm. By taking responsibility for our most important relationships, we create Calm in our lives. Calm feels like **leadership is managing people and culture (Thrive)**. Leaders and their employees begin to have adaptability and resilience before a crisis. At this level, leadership occurs as **comfortable, routine, and meaningful**.

#REALTALK with Us

Result: Calm → Creation

This part or Conversation addresses the **Will (Actions)** using three steps: Identity → Reclamation → Sovereignty. Our leadership expands from one-on-one conversations to influencing and building community. Moving away from Complacency (good enough), we explore our identity and our past, understanding how it impacts the safety, openness, and creativity of others. By doing so, we can powerfully choose the identities and stories to keep as leaders of leaders.

By accepting and embracing our identity, we release old systems around victimhood, martyrdom, and control. Our leadership aspires to create individual and collective sovereignty, creating leaders who move forward with a shared vision.

The result is Calm → Creation. Very few leaders get to this level, but we can look at systemwide examples like crypto and food sovereignty for inspiration. By shifting to Creation, **leadership is building the shared future (Author)**, collaborating with other leaders, and freeing ourselves from the past. At this level, leadership occurs as **valuable, deep, and profound**.

WHAT'S NEXT?

Like our exercises at the end of each chapter, this book is designed to be actionable. To jumpstart your journey, I invite you to complete one or more Calls to Action:

Work with Me

Since starting this movement in 2018, I have transitioned into my next decade of work: bringing the lessons and frameworks from #REALTALK to all workplaces on the planet. As an innovation and mental health speaker, my mission is to help leaders **build the future of their organizations without burning out.** I also speak on disruptive technologies like Web3, metaverse, and AI, and make it relevant and actionable for people in their day to day.

In celebration of this book, there are Keynote Experiences available for purchase, where we can have signed books for your audience. I am always delighted to meet and support the leaders of today, one step at a time. If you are leading an organization or a team who can use this work, I'd love to talk to you at hello@cherryrosetan.com.

Download the Discussion Guide

Bringing real talk to your life can feel intimidating yet doable. Our team has prepared the Still Standing Discussion Guide with reflection questions and journal prompts to kickstart your journey: http://wearestillstanding.com. For those who want to engage in a group setting, this guide allows you to create book clubs to work through the lessons and exercises.

From our experience at #REALTALK, what matters is moving words into action. Real talk is a necessary condition of modern leadership: taking our integrity, compassion, and bravery into every conversation we have. With this Still Standing Discussion Guide, you will gain manageable wins to scale that momentum. Try it yourself or rally a few friends to do this with you!

Start with One Conversation

#REALTALK was not built in a day. Like the way athletes train their physical muscles, founders train their mental and emotional muscles. Our movement, which has impacted 40 000 leaders, started with *one* conversation. A single founder that I opened up to during my moment of struggle.

Once you finish this book, put it down and call someone: a colleague, a friend, or even a family member. Have a real conversation with them. #REALTALK with Us is essentially one conversation at a time, practiced over months or years in our communities and in our workplaces. With your toolbox of strategies, go out there and take action!

ACKNOWLEDGMENTS

I want to start by acknowledging Brad Feld, who has been an incredible ecosystem builder and a staunch advocate of mental health in the tech industry. Thank you for the wise and inspiring words in the foreword you so generously contributed, which will have impact in years to come.

Much thanks as well to my rockstar teams from Wiley, Video Narrative, and Candid Goat, who have supported me on this journey: Bill Falloon, Richard Samson, Patel Purvi, Mike Isralewitz, and Philo Antonie Mahendran on my book team; Chris West, Tasha Vanesse, and Aaron Miyashita on my video team; and Becky Sue Wehry, Kendra Cagle, and Cindy Cowherd on my website team. It was such a privilege to work with all of you, in having such real conversations about the stories that needed to be told and for creating a world-class brand around my body of work. I couldn't have done this without you.

Last but not least, I send my deepest thanks to our #REALTALK champions, supporters, and participants over the years. This book is made possible by your commitment to this cause and the 60 tech founders, investors, and executive directors who formed the First Wave: the first set of mental health stories we released publicly.

It is on the foundation of these Champion Stories that we birthed this movement. Through these heartfelt and courageous conversations, this work has been made real.

Abdullah Snobar	Janet Bannister
Alan Wilson	Jason Tafler
Alanna Harvey	Jay Rosenzweig
Amanda Munday	Jayson Gaignard
Ameer Rosic	Jeff Dennis
Ami Shah	Jennifer Couldrey
Andrew Peek	Jennifer Love
Angela Lee	John Mavriyannakis
Anna Mackenzie	JS Cournoyer
Ben Baldwin	Julie Sabine
Bruce Croxon	Kin Lee-Yow
Caterina Rizzi	Kunal Gupta
Dan Martell	Lisa Durnford
Dean Hopkins	Lori Casselman
Edwin Frondozo	Marie Chevrier
Elizabeth Caley	Matt Roberts
Erica Pearson	Matthew Helt
Eva Lau	Matthew Leibowitz
Eva Wong	Michael Hyatt
Evgeny Tchebotarev	Mike Shaver
Farhan Thawar	Navid Nathoo
Floyd Marinescu	Neil Wainwright
Howie Diamond	Rhea Mehta
James Wallace	Roger Chabra
Jane Wang	Russell Korus

Sam Duboc

Sheetal Jaitly

Steve Pereira

Steven Pulver

Sunny Ray

Tami Zuckerman

Usha Srinivasan

Vicki Saunders

Wes Hodges

Yanik Silver

ABOUT
THE AUTHOR

Fifth-generation entrepreneur Cherry Rose Tan is the Entrepreneur in Residence at the Schulich School of Business, based in Canada's third largest university, where she advises an ecosystem of 250 startups and 3000 members. She leads Advisory and Fundraising services, where Schulich founders have raised $60M in four years, while teaching three MBA courses on entrepreneurship.

With 18 years of experience in tech, innovation, and entrepreneurship, she has a reputation as the First Mover in several industries. Tan served as pre-seed investor of Paycase Financial, a Canadian blockchain pioneer that provides infrastructure to global markets. She was also a general partner at Renew Venture Capital, an early-stage firm focused on impact and under-represented founders.

Her previous company #REALTALK, the mental health movement for the tech industry, is known for being North America's first and largest platform on Entrepreneurial Mental Health. Specializing in working with C-Suite leaders, Tan grew the movement to 40 000 leaders and 70 national champions in four years, with a synonymous Top 14 Business podcast on iTunes as well.

As an innovation and mental health speaker, she works with clients to **ensure that leaders build the future of their organization, without burning out along the way.** Speaking to corporations, associations, and universities around the globe, Tan is adept at demystifying complex technologies and translating possibility into reality through her methodology Possibility Executed™.

Her companies have been featured on Forbes, Inc., The Globe and Mail, CBC, Nasdaq, Reuters, and Insider for being disrupters in their industries. She also sits on the boards for Wellspring and the Canadian Mental Health Association.

REFERENCES

CHAPTER 1

1. Digitalundivided (2020). ProjectDiane 2020: the state of black & latinx women founders. https://www.digitalundivided.com/reports/projectdiane-2020.
2. Renken, E. (2020). Most Americans are lonely, and our workplace culture may not be helping. *Shots, NPR* (23 January). https://www.npr.org/sections/health-shots/2020/01/23/798676465/most-americans-are-lonely-and-our-workplace-culture-may-not-be-helping.
3. Startup Snapshot (2023). *The untold toll: the impact of stress on the well-being of startup founders and CEOs.* https://startup-snapshot.com/wp-content/uploads/2023/03/Startup-Survey_Final.pdf.

CHAPTER 2

1. Kahneman, D. (2013). *Thinking, Fast and Slow*. New York: Farrar, Straus and Giroux.
2. Marks, H. (1993). The value of predictions, or where'd all this rain come from? https://www.oaktreecapital.com/docs/default-source/memos/1993-02-15-the-value-of-predictions-or-where-39-d-all-this-rain-come-from.pdf.

3. Strebulaev, I.A. and Gornall, W. (2015). How much does venture capital drive the US economy? Stanford Graduate School of Business (21 October). https://www .gsb.stanford.edu/insights/how-much-does-venture-capital-drive-us-economy.
4. Quantum Workplace and Fierce Conversations (2017). The state of miscommunication: 6 insights on effective workplace communication. https://www .quantumworkplace.com/fierce-conversations-effective-workplace-communi cation-miscommunication.
5. VitalSmarts (2016). Costly conversations: why the way employees communicate will make or break your bottom-line. https://www.prnewswire.com/ news-releases/costly-conversations-why-the-way-employees-communicate-will-make-or-break-your-bottom-line-300373350.html.
6. Bravely (2019). Understanding the conversation gap: why employees aren't talking, and what we can do about it. https://learn.workbravely.com/hubfs/ Understanding-the-Conversation-Gap.pdf.

CHAPTER 3

1. Freeman, M., Johnson, S.L., Staudenmaier, P.J. et al. (2015). Are entrepreneurs "touched with fire"? Unpublished Manuscript (17 April). https://michaelafree manmd.com/Research.html.
2. Friedman, S. (2022). Entrepreneurs are struggling with mental health– but where's the support? https://blog.hubspot.com/sales/entrepreneurs-are-struggling-with-mental-health-but-wheres-the-support.
3. Syed, N. (2020). Tech CEO calls out industry's overwork culture. Human Resources Director Canada (6 January). https://www.hcamag.com/ca/speciali zation/employee-engagement/tech-ceo-calls-out-industrys-overwork-culture/195739.
4. Thank you to Simon Bowen of the Models Method for helping craft this visual model of our work.
5. McLeod, S. (2023). Maslow's hierarchy of needs. *Simply Psychology* (last updated 21 March). https://www.simplypsychology.org/maslow.html.
6. Effron, L. (2016). Michael Jordan, Kobe Bryant's meditation coach on getting in the zone. ABC News (16 April). https://abcnews.go.com/Health/michael-jordan-kobe-bryants-meditation-coach-flow-ready/story?id=38175801.
7. Griffith, E. (2014). Why startups fail, according to their founder. *Fortune* (25 September). http://fortune.com/2014/09/25/why-startups-fail-according-to-their-founders/.

8. Sutton, J. (2020). How to apply the wheel of life in coaching. *Positive Psychology* (29 July). https://positivepsychology.com/wheel-of-life-coaching/.
9. Brooks, M. (2019). *Developing Swimmers*. Champaign, IL: Human Kinetics Publishers Incorporated.

CHAPTER 4

1. Schudel, M. (2020). Tony Hsieh, entrepreneur who made Zappos an online retail giant, dies at 46. *Washington Post* (28 November). https://www.washingtonpost .com/local/obituaries/tony-hsieh-dead/2020/11/28/9669a22a-3197-11eb-bae0-50bb17126614_story.html.
2. Au-Yeung, A. and David Jeans, D. (2020). Tony Hsieh's American tragedy: the self-destructive last months of the Zappos visionary. *Forbes* (4 December 4). https://www.forbes.com/sites/angelauyeung/2020/12/04/tony-hsiehs-american-tragedy-the-self-destructive-last-months-of-the-zappos-visionary.
3. Hatzius, J., Briggs, J., Kodnani, D. et al. (2023). Global economics analyst: the potentially large effects of artificial intelligence on economic growth. https:// www.key4biz.it/wp-content/uploads/2023/03/Global-Economics-Analyst_ -The-Potentially-Large-Effects-of-Artificial-Intelligence-on-Economic-Growth-Briggs_Kodnani.pdf.
4. Comaford, C. (2012). Got inner peace? 5 ways to get it now. *Forbes* (4 April). https://www.forbes.com/sites/christinecomaford/2012/04/04/got-inner-peace-5-ways-to-get-it-now.
5. Psychology Today (2023). First impressions. *Psychology Today*. https://www.psy chologytoday.com/ca/basics/first-impressions (accessed 10 April 2023).
6. Thompson, J. (2011). Is nonverbal communication a numbers game? *Beyond Words* (blog), *Psychology Today* (30 September). https://www.psychologytoday.com/ ca/blog/beyond-words/201109/is-nonverbal-communication-numbers-game.

CHAPTER 5

1. Kotashev, K. (2022). Startup failure rate: how many startups fail and why in 2023? *Failory* (blog) (last updated 14 December). https://www.failory.com/blog/ startup-failure-rate.

2. Hendricks, G. (2009). *The Big Leap: Conquer Your Hidden Fear and Take Life to the Next Level*. San Francisco: HarperOne.
3. Sutton, J. (2020). The 6 stages of change: worksheets for helping your clients. PositivePsychology.com (12 August). https://positivepsychology.com/stages-of-change.
4. Godin, S. (2007). *The Dip: A Little Book That Teaches You When to Quit (and When to Stick)*. New York: Portfolio.

PART II

1. Vital, A. (2012). Startup dirty laundry: conflicts that kill partnerships [infographic]. *Adioma* (blog) (17 December). https://blog.adioma.com/startup-dirty-laundry-conflicts-that-kill-partnerships-infographic.
2. Elkins, K. (2017). A man who studied 500 millionaires shares the most effective step to take to succeed. CNBC (30 June). https://www.cnbc.com/2017/06/29/napoleon-hill-studied-500-millionaires-and-shares-their-key-to-success.html.

CHAPTER 6

1. Embroker Team (2023). Cofounder conflict: resolving business dilemmas like a boss. *Embroker* (blog) (27 February). https://www.embroker.com/blog/cofounder-conflict-guide.
2. Gadoua, S.P. (2017). Can marriage survive when your child dies under your watch? *Contemplating Divorce* (blog), *Psychology Today* (22 June). https://www.psychologytoday.com/ca/blog/contemplating-divorce/201706/can-marriage-survive-when-your-child-dies-under-your-watch.
3. AssistiveWare (2023). What is AAC? https://www.assistiveware.com/learn-aac/what-is-aac (accessed 10 April).
4. Hitching, G. (2023). The emotion wheel: how to use it and master your emotions. Science of People. https://www.scienceofpeople.com/the-emotion-wheel-how-to-use-it-and-master-your-emotions (accessed 10 April).

CHAPTER 7

1. Hawkins, D.R. (1995). *Power vs. Force: The Hidden Determinants of Human Behavior*. Sedona, AZ: Veritas.
2. Dowd, K. (2024). A sector-by-sector guide to the gender gap among startup founders. https://carta.com/blog/gender-gap-by-sector-2023/.
3. Whitley, R. (2021). Alarming numbers around men's mental health indicate need for national response. CBC (28 January). https://www.cbc.ca/news/opinion/opinion-men-mental-health-1.5871935.
4. Priory (2022). Men's mental health: 40% of men won't talk to anyone about their mental health. https://www.priorygroup.com/blog/40-of-men-wont-talk-to-anyone-about-their-mental-health.
5. Karpman, S.B. (1968). Fairy tales and script drama analysis. *Transactional Analysis Bulletin* 7 (26): 39–43. https://dx.doi.org/10.13140/RG.2.2.35742.18240.
6. Klaassen, R. (2020). We really need to talk about WE's white-saviour problem. *HuffPost* (15 July). https://www.huffingtonpost.ca/entry/we-charity-volunteer-white-saviour_ca_5f0e0652c5b648c301f07314.
7. Center for the Empowerment Dynamic (2023). TED* (*the empowerment dynamic). Center for the Empowerment Dynamic. https://theempowermentdynamic.com/about (accessed 11 April 2023).
8. Bockarova, M. (2016). 4 ways to set and keep your personal boundaries. *Romantically Attached* (blog), *Psychology Today* (1 August 1). https://www.psychologytoday.com/us/blog/romantically-attached/201608/4-ways-set-and-keep-your-personal-boundaries.
9. Brown, B. (2012). *Daring Greatly: How the Courage to Be Vulnerable Transforms the Way We Live, Love, Parent, and Lead*. New York: Gotham.

CHAPTER 8

1. Nash, J. (2014). From sad to mad: how suppressing your sadness invites anger. *GoodTherapy Blog* (15 April). https://www.goodtherapy.org/blog/from-sad-to-mad-how-suppressing-your-sadness-invites-anger-0415145.

2. Colier, C. (2018). What is forgiveness and how do you do it? *Inviting a Monkey to Tea* (blog), *Psychology Today* (15 March). https://www.psychologytoday.com/ca/blog/inviting-monkey-tea/201803/what-is-forgiveness-and-how-do-you-do-it.

3. Luciani, J. (2015). Why 80 percent of new year's resolutions fail. *Eat + Run* (blog), *U.S. News and World Report* (29 December). https://health.usnews.com/health-news/blogs/eat-run/articles/2015-12-29/why-80-percent-of-new-years-resolutions-fail.

4. Mackay, H. (2017). Why "good enough" is never good enough. *The Business Journals* (11 September). https://www.bizjournals.com/bizjournals/how-to/growth-strategies/2017/09/why-good-enough-is-never-good-enough.html.

5. Girlboss (2019). The venture capital world has a problem with women of color. https://girlboss.com/blogs/read/venture-capital-woc-women-of-color.

6. Guynn, J. (2020). Airbnb launches initiative with color of change to root out racial discrimination on its platform. *USA Today* (15 June). https://www.usatoday.com/story/tech/2020/06/15/airbnb-black-color-change-racial-discrimination-bias/5346602002.

CHAPTER 9

1. Wealth Dynamics (2023). Wealth dynamics in a nutshell. Wealth Dynamics. https://www.wealthdynamics.com/ (accessed 11 April).

2. Saplakoglu, Y. (2019). FDA calls psychedelic psilocybin a "breakthrough therapy" for severe depression. Live Science (25 November). https://www.livescience.com/psilocybin-depression-breakthrough-therapy.html.

3. Stebbins, S. and Suneson, G. (2020). Jeff Bezos, Elon Musk among US billionaires getting richer during coronavirus pandemic. *USA Today* (1 December). https://www.usatoday.com/story/money/2020/12/01/american-billionaires-that-got-richer-during-covid/43205617.

4. Green, K. (2024). A major loss of income for mothers is driving Canada's record-low fertility. The Hub (3 May). https://thehub.ca/2024/05/03/major-loss-of-income-for-mothers-is-driving-canadas-record-low-fertility.

5. Coleman, A.L. (2019). What's intersectionality? Let these scholars explain the theory and its history. *Time* (29 March 29). https://time.com/5560575/intersectionality-theory.

6. Dewan, S. (2021). How racism and sexism intertwine to torment Asian-American women. *New York Times*, (18 March). https://www.nytimes.com/2021/03/18/us/racism-sexism-atlanta-spa-shooting.html.

7. Liu, S. (2021). Reports of anti-Asian hate crimes are surging in Canada during the COVID-19 pandemic. CTV News (18 March). https://www.ctvnews.ca/canada/reports-of-anti-asian-hate-crimes-are-surging-in-canada-during-the-covid-19-pandemic-1.5351481.

8. Mental Health America (2023). BIPOC mental health. Mental Health America. https://www.mhanational.org/bipoc (accessed 11 April).

9. Center for Addiction and Mental Health (2023). What is Womenmind? Center for Addiction and Mental Health (CAMH). https://www.camh.ca/en/get-involved/join-the-cause/womenmind (accessed 11 April).

CHAPTER 10

1. Harrison, O. (2021). What if the new dream job is no job at all? Refinery29 (4 March). https://www.refinery29.com/en-ca/2021/03/10346116/why-people-quitting-jobs-covid.

2. Rodriguez, G.R. (2020). The great pause: are you preparing for the post-pandemic renaissance? *Forbes* (27 December). https://www.forbes.com/sites/giovannirodriguez/2021/12/27/are-you-ready-for-the-post-pandemic-rennaissance.

3. Cigna (2022). *Cigna 360 global well-being survey: exhausted by work – the employer opportunity.* https://www.cignaglobalhealth.com/static/docs/pdfs/na/cigna-360-global-well-being-survey-2022-employer-opportunity.pdf.

4. Wellhub (2023). *Gympass state of work-life wellness report.* https://wellhub.com/en-us/resources/research/work-life-wellness-report-2024.

5. Harter, J. (2022). Is quiet quitting real? Gallup (6 September). https://www.gallup.com/workplace/398306/quiet-quitting-real.aspx.

6. Westfall, B. (2022). Change fatigue is making employee burnout worse. https://www.capterra.com/resources/change-fatigue-in-the-workplace/.

7. American Psychological Association (2023). Work in America survey: artificial intelligence, monitoring technology, and psychological well-being. https://www.apa.org/pubs/reports/work-in-america/2023-work-america-ai-monitoring.

8. Alcantara, C. (2021). Reddit's /r/wallstreetbets astronomical rise. *Washington Post* (29 January). https://www.washingtonpost.com/technology/2021/01/29/wallstreetbets-reddit-gamestop.

9. Akhtar, A. (2021). The GameStop hearing combines everything lawmakers love: grilling tech execs and pointing fingers at Wall Street greed. *Business Insider* (18 February 18). https://www.businessinsider.com/why-is-congress-investigating-gamestop-rally-reddit-robinhood-2021-2.

10. Mannie, K. (2024). Posters promoting "Steal From Loblaws Day" are circulating. How did we get here? Global News (26 April). https://globalnews.ca/news/10449334/steal-from-loblaws-day-posters-food-inflation/.

11. Ipsos (2023). Seven in ten gen Z and millennials say buying a home is more out of reach than their parents' generation. https://www.ipsos.com/en-ca/Seven-in-Ten-Gen-Z-Millennials-Say-Buying-Home-More-Out-of-Reach-Than-Their-Parents.

12. Prime Minster of Canada (2024). Canada's housing plan. https://www.pm.gc.ca/en/news/news-releases/2024/04/12/announcement-canadas-housing-plan.

13. Smee, M. (2024). A new registry of bad tenants – and some landlords too – is gaining traction in Ontario. CBC News (20 January). https://www.cbc.ca/news/canada/toronto/online-tenant-database-ontario-openroom-1.7088219.

14. Gaskell, A. (2023). Is 2023 the year of "third space" working? *Forbes* (16 March). https://www.forbes.com/sites/adigaskell/2023/03/16/is-2023-the-year-of-third-space-working/.

15. City of Toronto (2019). Land acknowledgement. City of Toronto (last updated February). https://www.toronto.ca/city-government/accessibility-human-rights/indigenous-affairs-office/land-acknowledgement.

16. Schulz, P. (2015). Introducing the information's future list. The Information (6 October). https://www.theinformation.com/articles/introducing-the-informations-future-list.

17. Mathur, P. (2020). Quarterly VC funding for female founders drops to three-year low. PitchBook (8 October). https://pitchbook.com/news/articles/vc-funding-female-founders-drops-low.

18. Lorman (2021). 39 statistics that prove the value of employee training. https://www.lorman.com/blog/post/39-statistics-that-prove-the-value-of-employee-training.

19. Brende, B. (2019). We need a reskilling revolution. Here's how to make it happen. https://www.weforum.org/agenda/2019/04/skills-jobs-investing-in-people-inclusive-growth/.

20. Powell, J.A. (2017). Us vs them: the sinister techniques of "othering" – and how to avoid them. *The Guardian* (8 November). https://www.theguardian.com/inequality/2017/nov/08/us-vs-them-the-sinister-techniques-of-othering-and-how-to-avoid-them.

CHAPTER 11

1. Dickler, J. (2021). More colleges make covid vaccines mandatory for students. CNBC (12 April). https://www.cnbc.com/2021/04/12/covid-vaccines-increasingly-mandatory-at-colleges-this-fall.html.
2. Rosenfield, K. (2019). The real problem with cancel culture. *Tablet* (15 October). https://www.tabletmag.com/sections/news/articles/real-problem-with-cancel-culture.
3. Oak Engage (2023). *Employee dissatisfaction: survey reveals 74% say their leaders lack empathy in addressing resistance to change.* https://www.oak.com/newsroom/employee-dissatisfaction-survey-reveals-74-say-their-leaders-lack-empathy-in-addressing-resistance-to-change/.
4. Ewenstein, B., Smith, W., and Sologar, A. (2015). Changing change management. McKinsey (1 July). https://www.mckinsey.com/featured-insights/leadership/changing-change-management.
5. Scott, A., Klein, F.K., and Onovakpuri, U. (2017). Tech leavers study. Kapor Center for Social Impact (April). https://www.kaporcenter.org/wp-content/uploads/2017/08/TechLeavers2017.pdf.
6. Dastin, J. and Dave, P. (2021). Google AI scientist Bengio resigns after colleagues' firings: email. Reuters (6 April). https://www.reuters.com/article/us-alphabet-google-research-bengio-idUSKBN2BT2JT.
7. ZenBusiness (2023). New ZenBusiness research finds class of 2023 sees neurodiversity as an asset in leadership and is primed to be the most entrepreneurial. https://www.businesswire.com/news/home/20230614082058/en/New-ZenBusiness-Research-Finds-Class-of-2023-Sees-Neurodiversity-as-an-Asset-in-Leadership-is-Primed-to-be-the-Most-Entrepreneurial.
8. Sovrin (2018). What is self-sovereign identity? Sovrin (6 December). https://sovrin.org/faq/what-is-self-sovereign-identity.
9. BBC (2021). Poland abortion ban: thousands protest for third day. BBC (29 January). https://www.bbc.com/news/world-europe-55866162.

10. Food Secure Canada (2023). What is food sovereignty? Food Secure Canada. https://foodsecurecanada.org/who-we-are/what-food-sovereignty (accessed 11 April).
11. Royal Bank of Canada (2018). Humans wanted: how Canadian youth can thrive in the age of disruption. Royal Bank of Canada (March). https://www.rbc.com/dms/enterprise/futurelaunch/_assets-custom/pdf/RBC-Future-Skills-Report-FINAL-Singles.pdf.
12. Deloitte Insights (2020). Inclusive Work: Marginalized Populations in the Workforce of the Future. Deloitte Insights. https://www2.deloitte.com/content/dam/insights/us/articles/6587_DI-Inclusive-work/DI-Inclusive-work.pdf.
13. Low, J. (2014). *How the PayPal mafia redefined Silicon Valley*. http://www.thelowdownblog.com/2014/07/how-paypal-mafia-redefined-silicon.html.

CHAPTER 12

1. Ferry, K. (2015). Attracting and retaining millennials in the competitive hospitality sector. https://www.kornferry.com/insights/this-week-in-leadership/attracting-and-retaining-millennials-in-the-competitive-hospitality-sector.

INDEX

Intersectionality, 20, 165–169

The Iron Claw (film), 141

Jaitly, Sheetal, 145, 228

John Wick (film series), 141

Justice, 145, 185–186, 190, 205, 206

Kahneman, Daniel, 20

Kapor Center, 201

Karim, Jawed, 209

Karpman, Stephen, 125, 127

Kubler-Ross, Elisabeth, 61–62

La Via Campesina, 205

Labeling, 48, 95, 109–112

Large language models, 202

Leaders of leaders. *See also* Founders

  as authors, 157–158

  burnout in, 43, 108–109, 215

  in cancel culture, 200

  in collective ownership culture, 223

  and collective why, 230

  in communities, 150–151

  creating, 212

  definition of, 27–28

  effects of quitting on, 179

  empowerment by, 198–199

  as futurists, 33

  health of, 115

  and innovation, 52, 67

  and justice, 186

  as listeners, 69

  in mastermind structure, 98

  mental health issues of, 39

  performative nature of, 187

  and reclamation, 176, 184, 191–198

  relationships of, 163

  resentment in, 136–137

  and resilient, smart design, 206

  resistance to change by, 81–82

  and responsibility, 105

  self-care of, 45–47

  shame of, 121

  standards for, 76

  strategies for, 44

  support for, 210, 214

  as thought leaders, 153–154

  transformation by, 71, 230–231

  trauma in, 101–102

  uncertainty in, 49

  and Upper Limit Problem, 84

  and workability, 86, 201

Leadership. *See also* #REALTALK
    Leadership model

  addressing problems with, 145–146

  and avoidance, 57

  boundaries for, 130

  coaching for, 208, 209–210

  and communication, 163

  and community, 153, 195

  compassionate, 128

  core values of, 162

  as creation, 158

  effective, 31–32

and emotion, 134
and employee retention, 201
empowering, 122
fragility in, 107, 115
holistic, 55
importance of, 18–20
intentional, 167
lack of, 27
of masterminds, 98
and real talk, 221–222
reclaiming, 192, 196
and resentment, 138
responsible, 40, 94
self-, 64, 71–73, 85, 96, 127
and self-care, 47
and sovereignty, 205, 207
and three conversations, 36–37
and unraveling, 160–161
of VCs, 25
women in, 187–188
Lil Nas X, 190
Limited partners (LPs), 24
LinkedIn, 209
Listening:
    to affirmations, 215
    business value of, 69–71
    compassionate, 12, 134
    from empty, 74, 87
    fear of, 140
    and feedback, 133
    and identity, 162, 164, 194
    impact of, 192
    importance of, 67–69

receiving messages during, 86
resistance to, 114
and speaking, 71–73
willingness to, 118
without boundaries, 130
Lone wolves, 10–12, 115, 119, 161, 194
Long-term wins, 225–226
Loops, 83, 85, 143
Love and Belonging, 52
LPs (limited partners), 24
Luskin, Fred, 72
Lütke, Tobias, 46–47

McKinsey, 200
Maintenance, 84
Map of Consciousness, 119
Mapping the Margins (Crenshaw), 165
Marks, Howard, 23
Martyrs, 39–40, 91, 98, 125, 136, 161, 206, 233. *See also* Rescuers
Maslow, Abraham, 51–52
Maslow's Hierarchy of Needs, 52, 58, 204, 232
Masterminds, 5, 98, 194
MastermindTalks, 4–5
Maverick1000, 30
Max, Tucker, 5
Mehrabian, Albert, 73
Men's mental health, 123–125
Mental Health America, 168
Mentors. *See also* Advisors; Coaches
    in advisory mix, 209
    barriers to access, 176

financial, 6, 10
as influence, 106
and intersectionality, 20
of labeling, 109–111
of leaders of leaders, 27
of listening, 71
of real talk, 32
and shame, 120–121
and sharing, 130
of workability, 82, 85
Power vs. *Force* (Hawkins), 119, 121
Pre-contemplation, 84
Pre-revenue, 25
Prefrontal cortex, 48
Preparation, 76, 84
Prochaska, James, 84
Psilocybin, 160–161
Psychographics, 162–163, 206
Psychology Today, 143
PTSD (post-traumatic stress
    disorder), 160
Push-off, 59

Quantum Workplace, 27
Quiet quitting, 178–179, 184

Rabois, Keith, 209
Racism:
  at Airbnb, 145
  mitigation of, 206
  performative nature of, 187
  in tech industry, 33, 122

towards Black women founders, 166
towards Indigenous peoples, 185
trauma from, 140
and unraveling, 160, 166,
    185, 187, 206
Rage. *See also* Anger; Change rage
ceremonies for, 147
discontent as, 4
and grief, 101
healing through, 117
labeling, 111
over food security, 182–183
over housing affordability, 183–184
and reclamation, 181, 195
Reaction:
awareness vs., 107
during chaos, 50
dialog as cause of, 68
fear as, 49
in impostor syndrome, 65
moving from, 115
responding vs., 86, 232
#REALTALK Leadership model, 50–52,
    86, 119, 138–139, 157–158, 203.
    See also Leadership
#REALTALK with Cherry Rose Tan
    podcast, 147, 155
#REALTALK with Me conversation,
    40, 76, 86, 89, 95, 104, 232
#REALTALK with Us conversation:
  and authorship, 157–158
  calmness through, 233–234